Matthew Russell

Saint Joseph of Jesus and Mary:

Priedien Papers in his Praise

Matthew Russell

Saint Joseph of Jesus and Mary:
Priedien Papers in his Praise

ISBN/EAN: 9783744646789

Printed in Europe, USA, Canada, Australia, Japan

Cover: Foto ©Lupo / pixelio.de

More available books at **www.hansebooks.com**

SAINT JOSEPH

OF

JESUS AND MARY

Priedieu Papers in his Praise

BY THE

Rev. MATTHEW RUSSELL, S.J.

EDITOR OF "SAINT JOSEPH'S ANTHOLOGY"

"Joseph vir Mariae, de qua natus est Jesus."—Matt. i. 16

DUBLIN

M. H. GILL AND SON

50 Upper O'Connell Street

1898

Nihil Obstat:

G. H. MURPHY, S. T. D.

CENS. THEOL. DEPUT.

Imprimatur:

✠ GULIELMUS

ARCHIEP. DUBLINEN. HIBERNIÆ PRIMAS.

Die 16 Mens. Junii, 1898.

PREFACE

I HAVE found it very hard to choose a name for this new book about St. Joseph, and the name chosen at last needs an excuse. It was suggested by a story that is told of one of his most devoted clients, whose greatest glory is perhaps the part she has had in promoting the glory of St. Joseph. Our Lord, it is said, appeared one day to St. Teresa in the form of a child, and asked her name. " I call myself Teresa of Jesus." "And I," said the Divine Child, " call Myself Jesus of Teresa." Copying this model, I have dared to call the subject of this book St. Joseph of Jesus and Mary.

My title-page goes on to describe the book as made up of " priedieu papers " about St. Joseph. Some of them have appeared in *The Irish Monthly*, in the series of short and simple essays on spiritual subjects to which that name is given in the magazine—a name taken from the French word for *genuflexorium* or praying-stool. The word is included in Webster's English Dictionary, and defined " a kind of desk at which to kneel for prayer." It may be so far naturalised among us as to be pronounced *preedew*, without trying to bring out the French sound exactly. Some such local arrangement to remind us of our duty of morning and night prayer, and to help us at our prayers, might well be an item of bedroom furniture in a Catholic household.

In French periodicals the editorial responsibility is sometimes limited in these terms: *Pour les articles non signés le Gérant.* I might, by a similar formulary, make myself responsible for all that follows in these pages, whenever there is no other signature attached. There is an exception, however: the two opening papers I owe to kind and gifted friends—the first to the Very Rev. P. A. Sheehan, P.P. of Doneraile, and the second to Father John Fitzpatrick, O.M.I. And yet their names are not appended: first, because I have been allowed to make changes and adaptations for which the writers are not responsible; and, secondly, in order that my book might not have, from the start, the appearance of being less original, more of a compilation, than it really is. Even these items, like most of the verses in the Appendix, are original in the sense of being now published for the first time as a fresh tribute of affectionate devotion to St. Joseph.

The collection of original and selected " Poems in praise of the Foster-father " of our Divine Redeemer, which was published a year ago under the name of

Saint Joseph's Anthology, has received a warm welcome from the clients of the Saint. And now again I venture to offer to them a prose book written in his honour, which may perhaps win readers not only for itself but for its companion volume. Something may happen like what happened to two little boys, who, with older folk, once climbed up a certain Croagh Shee with straw hats on their heads. One of these hats was blown suddenly away out of sight down the stony side of the mountain, and was lost to view behind some rock or within some little hollow. None of the party could tell exactly in what direction it had gone, and therefore someone proposed that the other straw hat should be allowed to fly away too, but that its course should be watched very carefully. So was it done, and both hats were recovered. After I had in my mind applied this little autobiographical incident to this second book about St. Joseph, which I send after *Saint Joseph's Anthology*, I find that Shakespeare has forestalled me in the first scene of "The Merchant of Venice."

> "In my school days, when I had lost one shaft
> I shot his fellow of the self-same flight
> The self-same way with more advisèd watch,
> To find the other forth; and by adventuring both
> I oft found both."

Perhaps, somewhat in the same way, those for whom *Saint Joseph's Anthology* has hitherto been practically lost may be led to discover it by means of this further tribute of praise to our amiable Patriarch.

It would have been easy to break up these papers into the more usual form of a series of meditations, but I think that many would prefer to have them in their present unconventional and informal arrangement. The " Thoughts for St. Joseph's Day and for St. Joseph's Month " will serve for any day and any month when we may be drawn to pay special homage to the holy Spouse of our Immaculate Mother, to the Foster-father of our Divine Redeemer, to the Protector of the Universal Church, to the Patron of a happy death. For all that we want is a happy death. May our death bear a far-off likeness to thine, O St. Joseph of Jesus and Mary !

M. R.

May 1st, 1898.
Third Sunday after Easter,
Feast of St. Joseph's Patronage.

Saint Joseph of Jesus and Mary! I dare
To give thee that name, and to pray this bold prayer:
May I too be theirs, and oh! may I be
For ever, for ever, with them and with thee!

The Virgin of Avila, praying one day
In her convent, saw suddenly near her, they say,
Our Saviour Himself in the guise of a child,
Who eagerly ran to the maiden, and smiled,
Looking up at her fondly: "Pray, tell me your name."
"Teresa of Jesus I venture to claim."
"And Jesus am I of Teresa," He said.
Oh, how her heart glowed as the sweet vision fled!

"Teresa of Jesus." Her love urged this claim
To be His, and His only, in heart and in name.
But he whom Teresa has praised best of all,
The Saint whom the patron of deathbeds we call—
The Saint whom Teresa has taught us to love
And to trust, all the rest of God's servants above—
He, humble and lowly, can yet not disclaim
A still more endearing magnificent name.

Saint Joseph of Jesus and Mary! I dare
To give thee that name, and to pray this bold prayer:
May I too be theirs, and oh! may I be
For ever, for ever, with them and with thee.

M. R.

CONTENTS

SAINT JOSEPH

OF

JESUS AND MARY

———◆———

DEVOTION TO SAINT JOSEPH: THE COURSE OF ITS DEVELOPMENT

As the life of St. Joseph was a hidden life upon earth, so devotion to St. Joseph, deep and ardent though it always has been, was hidden in the Church for centuries. The veneration and affection has indeed been displayed more openly in these later ages, but it was reserved for Pius IX. — Pius, the priest of the Sacred Heart, and the preacher of Mary's privileges—to bring St. Joseph still more prominently before the faithful, thus reuniting, as it were, in the eyes of the faithful, the Sacred Trinity upon earth, the Holy Family of the house of Nazareth, Jesus and Mary and Joseph. In the Apostolic Decree which constituted St. Joseph patron of the Universal Church, it is stated "that the Church has always most highly honoured and praised the most Blessed Joseph, next to his Spouse the Virgin Mother of God, and has besought his intercession in time of trouble."

The development of doctrine and devotion in the Church, however, was necessarily very slow. For centuries the whole attention of the Church was directed to maintaining the true doctrines about the Incarnation. This was the fundamental truth of Christianity, and this was the most frequently and violently attacked. The God-Man, given by His own love and the charity of the Father to the Church, was the precious treasure upon which, during the early years of her existence, all her attention was lavished. All the marvellous mysteries wound round that central mystery of the Incarnation had to be explained ; and all the attacks, open and insidious, that sought to detract from the truth of that mystery, and the honour of God, had to be repelled. By degrees, when those controversies on the Incarnation had subsided, and the Church had a breathing-time, without ever forgetting her Spouse the Son, she directed her attention to the Mother; and by degrees, thinking them over first in her own deep mind, she put before her children truth after truth, and dogma after dogma, about the Mother,—her royal dignity, her Divine Maternity, her rich prerogatives, — until, in our own age, she reached the primary truth of all, that the Mother had never known sin, and the reality of her position was recognised—a Virgin and sinless. "And thus," as a holy priest has written, "the adoration of Jesus and the devotion to Mary took their places immovably in the sense of the faithful, and in the practical system of the Church ; one shedding light upon the other, and both instructing, illuminating, nourishing and sanctifying the people."

The claims of the All-Holy Son and His Virginal Mother being satisfied, the Church was able to turn her attention to the guardian of both, the father of the household at Nazareth. We have said that the Church is a type of Mary, and there can be no doubt that Mary is a teacher of the Church. When, therefore, the truth of her Son's Incarnation was placed beyond doubt, and any honour paid to St. Joseph could not prejudice the Divine Origin of her Child, the Church of God learned from her teacher's lips the dignity and the holiness of Joseph, and gathered from her heart deep feelings of love and gratitude to him. Mary's Divine Maternity protected and confirmed the truth of our Divine Lord's origin ; but, by a wise decree, the Church did not publicly preach the dignity of St. Joseph until the truth of the Incarnation was put beyond the cavils of heretics, lest the presence of St. Joseph might prejudice the exclusive right of the Eternal Father to the paternity of the Son. Devotion to an earthly father, even though he were only foster-father, might have given the enemies of Jesus Christ a pretence for denying His eternal generation from the Father; we must not, therefore, be surprised to find that public devotion to St. Joseph was not established in the Church as early as devotion to the Blessed Virgin, because the honour of our Divine Lord is to be maintained, whoever should suffer; and whereas Mary's Divine Motherhood was the surest protection of the honour of the Son, devotion to St. Joseph would have been seized upon by captious heretics as a proof that the Church was regardless of that first truth of the Incarnation, that Christ had no earthly father—as St. Athanasius declares — "Born of the Father before all ages, born of a Mother in time."

But although the Church's devotion to St. Joseph was not explicitly declared until the thirteenth century, there can be no doubt that his claims to the reverence of the faithful were fully acknowledged even in the earliest ages. It is to the East that common opinion traces the origin of devotion to St Joseph.   Before St. Athanasius, in the fourth century sent missionaries into Abyssinia to instruct the Copts in the rites of the Church of Alexandria, the sojourn of the Holy Family in Egypt was commemorated in Abyssinia, and a special festival was kept in honour of St. Joseph.   So, too, amongst the Christians of Syria, so ancient is the devotion that there is no record of its introduction amongst them.   There can be no doubt, too, that in the Greek Church the devotion is of great antiquity, as may be gathered from their hymns, and the custom that everywhere prevailed in Greece of calling children by the name of Joseph.

The history of the introduction of devotion to St. Joseph into the West is instructive. Father Faber, indeed, is of opinion that the devotion sprang up in the West itself—in the South of France. " It rose," he says, " from a confraternity in the white city of Avignon, and was cradled by the swift Rhone, that river of martyr-memories that runs by Lyons and Arles, and flows into the same sea that laves the shores of Palestine. The land which the contemplative Magdalen had consecrated by her hermit life, and whence the songs of Martha's school of virgins had been heard praising God, and where Lazarus had worn a mitre instead of a grave-cloth : it was there that he, who was so marvellously Mary and Martha combined, first received the glory of his devotion."

There can be no doubt now, however, that the great majority of ecclesiastical writers trace the devotion to the East, and attribute its introduction into Europe to the Carmelite Order, who came to the Western Church under the pontificate of Honorius III., in the first quarter of the thirteenth century. Half a century had not gone by when devotion to the earthly guardian of our Divine Lord had spread

2

through the universal Western Church. A century later, the greatest doctors of the Church exerted all their learning and eloquence to propagate this devotion to St. Joseph. Albertus Magnus, the teacher of St. Thomas, composed an office in his honour ; before his time, another Dominican, Brother Bartholomew of Trent, had written his biography. In 1416, whilst the Council of Constance was sitting, and the legates of the Holy See, twenty cardinals, two hundred bishops, and all the doctors and theologians of the Church, were earnestly debating the best means to stem the torrent of corruption that was devastating the Church, Gerson, the Chancellor of the University of Paris, appeared before the Fathers, and suggested devotion to St. Joseph as the most effectual remedy for the evil ; because, he argued, St. Joseph was the guardian of Christ, and he whom Christ obeyed on earth still retains an authority of affection over Christ in heaven ; and thus his wishes, like the wishes of Mary, are commands, and his intercession is all-powerful. His words were received as the words of one who had a mission from Heaven; and, in truth, according as devotion to St. Joseph spread in the Church, the troubles of the Church, one by one, disappeared. In less than a year, perfect peace was restored ; the distractions of schism and dissension ceased, and under the mild patronage of St. Joseph, the ever-

suffering Church had its history of persecution broken
by a momentary peace, which she seldom, and only
at rare intervals, enjoys.

Time went on, and now it was not a passing
schism, but the most fearful heresy that desolated
the Church; it was not a spark of hell-fire, but an
eruption; but devotion to St. Joseph lived and was
fostered in the Church by the greatest of his devoted
clients, St. Teresa; and when many of the nations of
Europe rejected Christ by rejecting His Church, the
Child and His Foster-father passed away into heathen
lands; and as at the passing of the Child in his father's
arms into Egypt, the idols trembled and fell, so
heathenism disappeared where the gospel of Jesus
was preached by His priests, and whole kingdoms
were evangelised and won over to God. "The
contemplative," says Father Faber, "took up the
devotion, and fed upon it; the active laid hold of
it, and nursed the sick, and fed the hungry in its
name. The working people fastened upon it, for
both the Saint and the devotion were of them. The
young were drawn to it, and it made them pure;
the aged rested on it, for it made them peaceful.
St. Sulpice took it up, and it became the spirit of
the secular clergy; and when the great Society of
Jesus had taken refuge in the Sacred Heart, and the
Fathers of the Sacred Heart were keeping their
lamp burning, ready for the resurrection of the

Society, devotion to St. Joseph was their stay and consolation. . . So it gathered into itself orders and congregations, and high and low, young and old, ecclesiastical and lay, schools and confraternities, hospitals, orphanages, and penitentiaries, everywhere holding up Jesus, everywhere hand in hand with Mary, everywhere the refreshing shadow of the Eternal Father. Then, when it had filled Europe with its odour, it went over the Atlantic, plunged into the damp umbrage of the backwoods, embraced all Canada, became a mighty missionary power, and tens of thousands of savages filled the forests and the rolling prairies at sundown with hymns to St. Joseph, the praises of the Foster - father of our Lord."

Such is a brief outline of the history of this wonderful devotion. And such is the way that God has chosen to recompense the Protector of Jesus and Mary. The hidden life of Nazareth is changed for the glory of Heaven, and the worship of God's Church upon earth. The meek and lowly Joseph is Patron of the Universal Church. So deep was his humility upon earth, that he seems to us to have been no more than the unconscious agent of the miracles of Heaven, and he little knew that for the fulfilment of the high functions God had entrusted to him his soul had been fitted with transcendent virtues; and that in after ages learned doctors of the Church would study eagerly his life and his character, knowing well that in both they would discover traces of the spiritual omnipotent work of the Holy Spirit. He must have been completely unconscious of his sanctity during life, and now we have saints far advanced in spiritual life sitting at his feet to learn sanctity, for they know that he, who on earth and in heaven is nearest to Christ, is likest unto Christ, and that to be like unto Joseph is also to be like unto Jesus. Who was more humble, more hidden, than the carpenter of Nazareth? Yet, behold, the great wisdom of the Church does not separate him in glory from those with whom he was associated in misery, but throughout the Church devotion to St. Joseph is spreading, laying hold of all hearts, and subduing them; not the hearts only of the young, or the poor and the lowly, whose life is like to his, but even saints, as I have said, are happy to bring themselves under his sweet influence; and mighty schemes for the sanctification of souls are placed under his protection, and difficult problems are submitted to him for solution, and grave doctors have often appealed to the Foster-father of Jesus for guidance and assistance. Among many other edifying traits of character, it is recorded of a great theologian of our time, that oftentimes, when burdened with anxious care, he has been seen to lay his head on the feet of St. Joseph, as if appealing to the

Protector of our Divine Lord for light and strength
to guard the mystic body of Christ as Joseph guarded
Jesus from His enemies on earth.

When the holy and amiable Pius IX. was Pope,
there was a great artist in Rome who received an
order to paint a picture commemorative of the pro-
clamation of the dogma of the Immaculate Concep-
tion. The scene of the picture was partly laid in
heaven, and, skilful as he was, the artist had great
difficulty in grouping round the Heavenly Throne
the many choirs of saints and angels. When the
outline of the painting had been made, he took it to
the Vatican for the Pope's approbation. Throwing a
quick glance over the sketch, the Holy Father
detected an omission. "And St. Joseph—where is
he?" "I will put him there," said the artist, point-
ing to a group lost in clouds of light and glory.
"Not so," said the Holy Father, "but "—laying his
finger by the side of our Divine Lord—"you will put
him *there*, for that is his place in heaven."

THE ESPOUSALS OF SAINT JOSEPH

THE earliest annual feast of St. Joseph is celebrated on the twenty-third day of the first month of the year. In the calendar it is called indeed the Espousals of the Blessed Virgin Mary; but it is his rather than hers, it is the beginning of his greatness. As in the Gospel her glory is summed up in being called " the Mother of Jesus," so his is summed up in being called "the husband of Mary." All his life long God was preparing him, though he knew it not, for his great wedding-day; thenceforth all his graces would come to him, and he knew it, because of that day's grace. It was precisely because of his conjugal relationship to her that, to her eyes, he became, in a few months' time and from the moment of the Incarnation, the visible proxy of her invisible Spouse, the Holy Ghost, and the shadow of the Eternal Father; and that, to the eyes of men, a little later, he would pass for the father of her only Son, who was also the only-begotten Son of God.

It was, says Suarez, soon after the opening of her fourteenth year, which was the marriageable age among her people, that the Blessed Virgin's Espousals took place. There can be but little doubt that at the time St. Joseph was still in the prime of life, say between thirty and forty years of age, the limit which the majority of great minds in modern times would put to his years. The opinion of Mary of Agreda,—a holy nun who had the gift of saying most beautiful things about Our Lady and all her concerns,—which numbers his years as thirty-three, seems to have much to recommend it. At all events, we may take it for certain that St. Joseph was not the old man whom, in the olden times, painters and theologians alike were so fond of depicting, and we may safely conclude that he was not more than fifty years of age.

Mary was probably an orphan at this period ; and her marriage, as was customary in such cases, was arranged for her by her guardians among the priests of the Temple, in which, for about eleven years, as tradition assures us, she had been brought up. Some authors think it was by a special inspiration of Divine Providence that Joseph the carpenter was chosen for so high an office ; but, be this as it may, we know from the event that he was the chosen of God, and that that marriage at least was made in heaven. The old legend, which tells how the many suitors for the maiden's hand were weeded out until the one perfect flower of purity was left, represents the choice as being made pretty much as Aaron was elected to the priesthood in the grey ages long before; the dried wands of the aspirants having been left in the Temple overnight, it was found in the morning that Joseph's almond-branch had budded into flower. A letter attributed to St. Jerome lends countenance to the story; and, whatever may be thought of its historical character, it is true at least with the "true truth" of things.

Being an only child, and so an heiress, though doubtless her earthly heritage was not much more than her father's house at Nazareth—the Holy House that was to be—and its immediate surroundings, she is bound to marry, since marry she must, a man of her own tribe and family. That she was of the tribe of Judah and of the royal house of David is evident, from what is said of her Divine Son in prophecy and Gospel alike; while, on the other hand, the Gospel genealogies show clearly that Joseph was of the same illustrious pedigree. Heiress she was of the blood royal, which, in her case only and in His who was to be born of her, was unsullied at its source with the least stain of sin; and her blood was to end right royally in the Precious Blood of that Son of David, whom long ago David had called his Lord.

But Mary's true dowry was other than this. A few months after her Espousals she is saluted by the Angel of the Annunciation as "full of grace;"

and even now, we may be sure, she is as full of grace as can be, though her capacity was always growing, especially from that day forth, until the end. She is the heiress too, the sole heiress of the hopes of Israel, which, still unfledged, are stirring in her heart like young doves in the nest.

Ah! she was indeed a fit spouse for Joseph; she who, as a little time would show, was a fit spouse for God. For, as old "Anthony Stafford, Gent." (a Protestant) says in his book, *The Femall Glory*: "The bonds of her matrimony were already askt in Heaven, and no impediment was found why she might not wedde God Himself." And Joseph was a not unfitting husband for such a wife, chosen as he was, for the father that was dead, by her Father who was in heaven. What he was already we can judge—though, of course, his holiness would grow and grow from his daily intercourse with Mary—from the fact that, with regard to the Divine event that was soon to follow, the Evangelist says emphatically that he was "a just man." Now love is a leveller, as we know, especially the love of God; and thus naturally, and supernaturally, Joseph, we may be sure, would have been Mary's own choice, if choice she had had, or had wished to make. Abbot Rupert, in his commentary on St. Matthew, says that the Holy Ghost, who dwelt both in Mary and in her virginal spouse, was the conjugal love that united them.

Pious fancy seems to behold the maiden as she moves to that high bridal; and memory recalls, as doubly true of her, what was written of the first, and as yet unfallen, Eve—

> "Grace was in all her steps, Heaven in her eye,
> In every gesture dignity and love."

And even these were but the outward signs of the inward grace of which her pure soul was full.

The reasons for this marriage are evident. As the martyr-poet of Shakespeare's time, Father Robert Southwell, S.J., rather naïvely put it—

> "In marriage knots to Joseph she was tied,
> Unwonted works with wonted veils to hide."

and again—

> "God lent His Paradise to Joseph's care,
> Wherein He was to plant the Tree of Life."

Already, indeed, had the coming event cast its graces before. As Mont Blanc, at dawn, takes the sunlight on his brow, while yet the neighbouring mountains are subjects of the night, so are the pure heights of the Espousals already lighted up from the clouded east of the Sacred Infancy, and there, hand in hand, Mary and Joseph are standing, clad in the white splendours of the unrisen Son of Justice.

But how can Mary enter into a true marriage-contract,—and it is certain from the Gospel that she did so,—being bound, as is generally believed, by a vow of perpetual virginity? That, at the time of the

Annunciation, she was so bound, is plain, as St. Augustine remarks, from her own words to the Angel. The Abbé Orsini, following Descoutures, thinks that her vow may be assigned to the early days of her orphanhood. The common opinion goes much further, and says that she consecrated herself irrevocably to God from her earliest years, probably at the time of her Presentation in the Temple. But St. Thomas Aquinas says, in the *Summa*, that though Our Blessed Lady had made a vow of chastity before her marriage, it was only on condition that such would be pleasing to God, and that it was only after her Espousals that she made, together with St. Joseph, an absolute vow of perpetual virginity.

It was fitting that she who was destined to be the Mother of God, should be the model of all His children; so, by her marriage, she was made the patroness of wives as well as of maidens. Her marriage was in some sort a sacrament before sacraments were known. To Mary herself it must have seemed more like the heavenly sacrament of the everlasting growth of glory, rather than the earthly, though Divine, sacrament of a special grace. For she had long been dear to the Holy Spirit of God, and rich in all the favours of His grace; and this was their betrothal. The Divine Espousals were soon to follow on this wedding-day, in her quiet home at Nazareth; and the day was not far distant when the

Eternal Word of God, become her little Babe, would preach, by the mute assurance of His presence, from the tiny pulpit of the Crib, what one day He would proclaim by word of mouth to the whole wide world, and even unto us : " Where there are two or three gathered together in My name, there am I in the midst of them."

THOUGHTS FOR SAINT JOSEPH'S DAY

"WHO, thinkest thou, is the faithful and wise steward whom the Lord setteth over His family?" It is our Lord Himself who has asked this question in the twelfth chapter of St. Luke; but He has not given to it there the peculiar meaning which the question must bear for us to-day. For this is the feast of St. Joseph.

The Church, indeed, grateful to the guardian of her Divine Redeemer and of His Immaculate Mother, has consecrated more than one day to his honour; and his devout clients have made this entire month the month of St. Joseph. But they have done so, they have honoured March with their choice for this purpose out of all the twelve months of the year, because this nineteenth day of March was already the first and chief of the festivals of St. Joseph.

Yes, this is St. Joseph's Day; and when to-day we ask ourselves, "Who is this faithful and wise steward whom the Lord setteth over His family?" we think of Bethlehem and of Egypt and of Nazareth, and our hearts answer, "St. Joseph!"

The whole human race is indeed the family of God.
Every child of Adam has a right to join in that
heaven-taught prayer which begins with "Our
Father." Almighty God is the common Father of
all, and towards each of His poor human creatures
His heart yearns with a Father's love. But there was
once on this earth a small and humble household
which in a much closer and more literal sense de-
served the title of God's family; for the Son of God
Himself was there, and His most Blessed Mother.

This was the grand central point in the world's
history, though the world knew it not. This was the
one supreme crisis to which all the prophets of the
Old Law looked forward, and to which all the saints
of the New Law look back. This was the sacred
group of three, so dear to devout contemplation
under the express name of the Holy Family, repro-
duced in so many beautiful paintings and so many
pious prints, and, better still, in the reality of so
many Christian homes. This was indeed God's
family, containing all that was dearest to God's
Heart, dearest and nearest and best in heaven and
upon earth. And we know "who was the faithful
and wise steward whom the Lord set over His
family to give them their measure of wheat in due
season," to toil for their support, to guard them from
their enemies, to be their solace, their sustenance, and
their defence.

If St. Joseph had been no more than this—if he had only been chosen from without, as a stranger might have been chosen, as holy Simeon might have been chosen, as that other Joseph of Arimathea or Joseph Barsabas, surnamed the Just, might have been chosen, to provide for the temporal wants of the Mother and the Child—he would even thus have been entitled to our deepest gratitude and reverence, and it would have been hard to go too far in honouring him whom the Almighty Lord of heaven and earth had deigned thus to honour.

But he was far more than this. " Joseph," says the Evangelist, "was the husband of Mary, of whom was born Jesus." This text is the very first word that the Church speaks in praise of St. Joseph in the office of his Feast ; this was the first antiphon of vespers yesterday with which this Feast began. For this is his supreme and all-sufficient title and dignity —"Joseph was the husband of Mary, of whom was born Jesus." Joseph, therefore, was the true Spouse of the true Mother of the true Son of God. He had all a father's authority, as far as any human creature could have, over the Son of God. God delegated to him the rights, the duties, and the privileges of a father.

No, it was not through mere courtesy, as it were, or in order merely to accommodate her language to the ignorance of those who knew not the mystery of the

Divine Incarnation, that the Blessed Virgin herself says of St. Joseph to her Divine Son: "Thy father and I have sought Thee, sorrowing." *Thy father!* In his relationship to our Lord, St. Joseph thus comes under the sanction of the Fourth Commandment— that least necessary of all the Divine precepts, which nevertheless God has placed first in the second table of the law, first among the precepts which regard, not God Himself, but our fellow-creatures: *Honour thy father and thy mother.* Now, Jesus, as He said, "came not to destroy, but to fulfil the law;" and if, in order to set for us a pattern of obedience, He conformed to ordinances which not only bound Him not, but which might seem unbefitting to His sanctity —if, for instance, He who had come to expiate sin submitted to the expiatory rite of circumcision, as if Himself a sinner—if His all-pure Mother presented herself for legal purification in the Temple, as if the sinful mother of a sinner—if Jesus in His obedience would thus obey all laws and fulfil all justice, how much more will He perfectly observe this sweet commandment of God's predilection: *Honour thy father and thy mother?*

Not Mary only, but Joseph also. She indeed is His true mother, more His mother than any woman is mother to the child of her bosom; but St. Joseph's claims come next to hers. And therefore for thirty years Jesus was subject to them both. *Erat subditus*

3

illis: to *them,* not to her alone. Nay, in a certain sense more subject to Joseph than to Mary; for he, not she, "was the faithful and wise steward whom the Lord had set over His family;" he, not she, was head of the Holy Family, the earthly minister and representative of the Eternal Father who is in heaven.

There is no need of long and deep meditation on the privileges of this glorious, hidden Saint, to convince us of the high place he holds in the hierarchy of heaven, and of the high place he ought to hold in our hearts. No, to justify fully the love and veneration and confidence which, thank God, we feel or wish to feel, and are trying and praying to feel, towards this glorious and most powerful and most amiable Patron of the Universal Church, nothing more is required than to think, even passingly as we are doing, yet seriously and in a spirit of faith and love, on all that is involved in the offices which were confided to him during his life on earth. For surely the highest earthly dignity, next to the Divine Maternity itself, consists in being thus chosen out of all the generations of men to enter into that mystic and virginal, but most true and real, nuptial union with the Blessed Virgin, which made St. Joseph much more than Foster-father by adoption to her Divine Son, our Lord and Saviour Jesus Christ. *Cum desponsata esset mater Jesu Maria Joseph:* "Mary the

Mother of Jesus, espoused to Joseph." Jesus, Mary, Joseph: the mere joining of these sacred names, the mere naming of this earthly trinity, is the only and the sufficient foundation for all the great things that can be said or thought about St. Joseph.

No wonder, then, at the great things which *have* been said of him. No wonder at the unbounded confidence in St. Joseph's intercession, which filled the hearts of St. Thomas Aquinas, of St. Bernard and St. Bernardine, of St. Francis de Sales ; above all, of St. Teresa and the pious Chancellor Gerson, and so many other saints canonised or uncanonised.

No wonder, indeed ; but the wonder rather is that greater honours were not sooner paid in the Church of Christ to this last of the Patriarchs and first of the New Testament Saints. Yes, the wonder is that our Divine Lord suffered His Church so long to conspire with the humility of His Foster-father, by letting the Hidden Life of Nazareth continue for him through so many Christian centuries, during which the holy Patriarch was brought forward far less prominently in the public devotions of the faithful than was manifestly demanded for him by his pre-eminent dignity and authority in the Holy Family on earth, and by his corresponding dignity and power in the Holy Family of the blessed in heaven.

Of the seeming neglect displayed towards this

hidden Saint for so many centuries, one reason may have been that the pious faithful could not think of him separately and apart from his Divine Lord; and he was thus lost and absorbed in the near brightness of the Sun of Justice—like those planets which are said to have escaped till now the search of the astronomers on account of the closeness of their orbits to the sun.

Father Faber speaks somewhere of this earth of ours as " this beautiful moonlit planet, third in order from the sun." Third in order, for it was supposed that only Mercury and Venus were closer than ourselves to the centre of light and heat. But science in our own day has dared to peer further into the brightness as well as further out into the dark; and she has not only discovered new planets upon " Creation's twilight-verge," where their remoteness from the sun, their dearth of light, had hidden them, but in the opposite direction also, nearer to the sun than even Mercury, planets have recently been discovered, concealed from our view till now by their very nearness to the sun and by their excess of light. Like those intra-Mercurial planets (as they have been sometimes called), St. Joseph might seem to have been hidden so long from the gaze of men by the very closeness of his relations with the Incarnate God.

But whatever may be the case with regard to St.

Joseph in the Church at large, how has it fared with
him in the Church of God which is within us? In
the temple of our hearts, has not the homage due to
St. Joseph been withheld, too long delayed, and then
paid in too niggardly a measure? Have we not
been too slow and too cold in recognising the full
strength of St. Joseph's claims upon our filial love
and allegiance? Heresy pretends to be scandalised
at the excess of our devotion to the saints; but,
alas! we know ourselves better. If the matter were
not so terribly serious, we might almost be amused
at the solicitude of this class of Protestants, and we
might say to one of them: " Really, my good friend,
you need not be so much alarmed. If you but
knew how seldom we think of St. Joseph (for
instance)—how seldom we pray to him, and, when
we do, how coldly—even *you* would be satisfied, and
you would see how very far we stop short of anything approaching to idolatrous worship. Ah! we
have not the slightest fear of going too far, and
we have a very great fear of not going nearly far
enough."

All this perhaps is particularly true of our habitual
attitude towards St. Joseph. Well, in whatever degree
we may have been wanting towards him hitherto, this
is a good time to arrange with ourselves, by the
help of God's grace, to cherish henceforth a very
tender, practical, personal devotion to the glorious

and amiable Saint to whom this day and this month are dedicated. True devotion to St. Joseph is chiefly shown by earnest and persevering effort to imitate his virtues hour by hour until the hour of our death.

St. Joseph is the Patron of hidden lives, of obscure virtues, of hard work and of happy deaths.

A happy death! We may ask St. Joseph to obtain for us other graces also, if we please, but our constant and most fervent petition must be for the crowning grace of a happy death. St. Joseph has been appointed the official guardian, so to speak, and special Patron of a happy death, because his own death was visibly blest beyond all others—with his dying head pillowed to the Heart of Jesus, and Mary bending over him lovingly and praying for him to the last.

And yet, in one respect, the deathbed of St. Joseph's devout client is happier than his own. St. Joseph's death was a parting from all that he loved, since he left Jesus and Mary behind him. But now the Christian's death is rather a meeting than a parting, a going home from this place of exile, this valley of tears ; for Jesus has gone before us to prepare a place for us (that is His own tender word), and the desire of His Heart is that where He is we also may be. At any moment the message may come for any one of us that "all things are ready." May that message find us ready! As we have often prayed, may Jesus, Mary, and Joseph help us in our dying hour ; for that hour, that moment, the moment of death, shall be followed by the judgment, in which our merciful Judge shall be Jesus the Son of Mary, the Foster-Child of our own St. Joseph. Oh, dear St. Joseph, pray to Jesus for us now and at the end, that He may then, to the very end, be our merciful Judge and our Saviour.

THOUGHTS FOR SAINT JOSEPH'S MONTH

MARCH is St. Joseph's month. Except, of course, May and the Blessed Virgin—and, as St. Augustine and the Council of Trent say of her with regard to sin, *she* is an exception everywhere—except the month of May, there is no special dedication of any of the months so universally recognised by the devout faithful as that which makes March the month of St. Joseph. One of the reasons sometimes put forward for the choice of May as Our Blessed Lady's month, is the utter dearth of her festivals at that fair season. At present, indeed, the 24th of May is the Feast of Mary, Help of Christians, but this is almost a thing of our own day. Though this title of Help of Christians was inserted in the Litany of Loretto by St. Pius V. in thanksgiving for Our Lady's share in the Christian victory at Lepanto in 1571, it was only in our nineteenth century that Pius VII., upon his return to Rome after so many trials and dangers, instituted the Festival of B.V.M. Auxilium Christianorum, having already shown his gratitude to the Queen of Heaven, whose help he had implored during his long imprisonment at Savona, by crowning her famous statue in that city with a golden crown, under the title of Mother of Mercy. With regard to St. Joseph, on the contrary, the fact that the 19th of March is his principal feast seems to have been the sole claim of the month of March to the glory of being marked out as that happy month out of all the twelve which shall, as the years slip past, be for ever linked thus closely with St. Joseph's name. But the ingenious piety of the faithful needed no very urgent excuse for desiring something new in honour of the holy Patriarch.

St. Joseph's month, and all that concerns St. Joseph, must be very dear to the Heart of Jesus ; for to the Heart of Jesus St. Joseph was dear from the first on earth, and grew dearer each day through his life—and what is he now in heaven ? At the beginning, in the very earliest throb of love that sent the precious blood more swiftly through the veins of the new-born Saviour, first after the Immaculate Mother, Joseph must have claimed his special share. Nay, that was not the beginning even on earth. And before earth itself began, " Devotion to St. Joseph " began—when in the everlasting councils of Infinite Wisdom the Almighty Father, looking forward out of the depths of His unbeginning eternity, singled St. Joseph out from all the generations of the sons of men to be the guardian and spouse of the purest, and highest, and best-beloved of His creatures, to be the guardian and Foster-father of His own Divine co-equal Son—image and representative to the one of her Divine Spouse, the Holy Ghost ; to the other, of His Father in heaven. When, before the Heart of Jesus had yet begun to beat, before Jesus was Jesus, before the world was yet made—when the Word in the bosom of the Father said, *Behold I come*, He meant to come as the Blessed Virgin's child, as the Son of her whose Spouse would be St. Joseph. It has been often said that when God chooses any of His poor creatures for some great and high end, His very choice endows them with gifts proportionate to their work and dignity. " It is by comparing God's choice of him with the office he was to fill, that we come to see the glory and the grandeur of St. Joseph, and to contemplate with reverent awe the heights of a holiness to which such familiarity with God was permitted." [1] The devout writer from whom we have taken these words, calls St. Joseph, in another work, the shadow of the Eternal Father. "This is the immensity of his dignity,—the incommunicable and ever-blessed paternity is in figure communicated to him. He is the Foster-father of Jesus. To the world without he passes for His father. He exercises the authority of a father over Him, and performs for

[1] F. Faber's *Precious Blood*, page 8. This spiritual writer is quoted more at length at page 86.

Him all the affectionate and anxious offices of a father. The unspeakable treasures of God, Jesus and Mary, are committed to St. Joseph's keeping; and he is himself a treasure as well as the treasure-house of God. He is part of the scheme of redemption. What wonder theologians should tell us such great things of his copious graces and his mighty gifts ? "

What wonder indeed ? And all this only as a *preparation* for the transcendent graces which filled every moment of the last twenty or thirty years of his life, for hardly anything has been said here except concerning the mere fact of God's original choice of St. Joseph, which mere fact, indeed, includes all. Yet the author of one of the best books on the glories of St. Joseph, Father Patrignani, does not rank this formally among his twelve motives for being devout to this last of the Patriarchs and first of the New Testament Saints. The first eight of these motives are the examples of Jesus Christ, of the Blessed Virgin, of the Holy Angels, of the Catholic Church, of princes, kingdoms, and cities, of religious orders, of many ascetic writers, and, finally, of many saints and eminently holy souls; and then follow four motives drawn from St. Joseph's peculiar greatness and goodness, generosity and power, as patron and protector of all Christians in all states and all emergencies of life, and, above all, in the awful moments of the last agony, which he helps so often to change into a happy death, like his own.

How many happy deaths there are taking place (please God) every day, all the world over! Ah! there are many, many deaths going on, too, that it is dismal to think of—but so many peaceful, holy, happy deaths! Even the physical pain of dying is probably exaggerated in the apprehensions of vigorous health, by our natural shrinking from dissolution. The soul and the body that are suffering the agony of that parting, are not in the same state as those of the pitying spectator. All the terrible things that are said and felt about death are hardly to be understood of the faithful Christian's deathbed. If there be special risks then, God gives special graces then also. And so, often, very often, the worst is over before the worst appears to have begun, and it seems at last like a gentle falling asleep, to be followed very soon by a happy awakening.

Now, in this sense, St. Joseph's death might be called the first Christian death. The saints, known and unknown, of the Old Law, indeed died in the faith and hope of the future Redeemer—in hope, but hope with a stern infusion of resignation, for He who was to come seemed far away. But except, perhaps, old Simeon and a few others, Joseph was the first to die with this hope warm and near to his heart; or rather, for him hope is changed into possession; for now He who *was* to come *has* come, and Joseph has clasped Him to his heart, and felt his Sacred Heart beating against his own.   And now, again, in turn his head is pillowed on the Heart of Jesus, and Mary bends over him lovingly, praying in her Immaculate Heart; and he dies happy, in the very lap of all that is holiest and most beautiful and divinest out of heaven.

Yet even he, the Patron of a happy death, might almost envy us the circumstances of our dying. In some respects our deathbed might even seem happier than St. Joseph's.   His death was, though only for a short space, yet a real parting, a taking leave of Jesus and Mary; ours, if we use aright His merciful graces to the end, will be but a going home to Jesus.   At least, when we are dying, the particular judgment is only a few days, or hours, or minutes, in front of us; and *that* will place us at the feet of Jesus.   Would not St. Joseph's death have been happier if Jesus had gone before him, as He has gone before to prepare for *us*?   Whatever was happiest in St. Joseph's happy death may be ours substantially in our lower measure.   When he came to die, when Jesus was to be more directly about His Heavenly Father's business, and His earthly father had given to Him and to His Blessed Mother all the loving service that was needed; when the Heart of Jesus was satisfied, and said: " It is enough—he is ready for his reward, he has attained a height of sanctity fit for the place which will belong in the glory of heaven, for all eternity, to him who has toiled so well and so long for Me and My Mother, and of whom My Mother once said to Me, ' *Thy father and I have sought Thee, sorrowing,'* "—when the inconceivable measure of his graces and his glories was thus filled up to that Divine Heart's content, then at last Jesus dismissed His most faithful servant and His nearest friend, according to His word, in peace ; and his eyes, closing calmly in death, " *saw their salvation,*" saw the Mother and the Son bending, with love and blessing and prayer, over him whom they loved so tenderly from the first and to the end, and whom they love so tenderly now this moment, and will for all eternity, in heaven. Did Jesus, who wept over Lazarus, and over the son of the Naim widow—did Jesus and Mary weep over this happy deathbed ? And how soon after was the Holy Household of Nazareth broken up, in order that Jesus may at length—how long He has waited, and how much He has taught us while waiting !—may at length " *be about His Father's business,*" and may "*go about doing good unto all*" ? For there is another deathbed at which Mary must assist ; and *there* her breast will not be allowed to pillow His dying head, but she must stand heartbroken by His Cross till death gives Him to her arms once more. Mary at one deathbed, Jesus and Mary at the other ;

at ours, Jesus and Mary and Joseph. Jesus will be there with His grace and in His Sacramental Presence, and Mary by her prayers ; and to these we shall join the third of the earthly trinity in praying, not for the first or the thousandth time, " Jesus, Mary, Joseph, help me in my last agony."

In life, then, and in death, let us have the holy names of Jesus and Mary and Joseph upon our lips and in our hearts. St. Joseph's greatness lies in the closeness of those names. St. Matthew, his special evangelist, whom alone we have to thank for the little that we know about him, has cunningly contrived to bring the three dear names together in his first chapter, without so much as a comma to separate them—*Cum esset desponsata mater Jesu Maria Joseph.* " *Whom God hath joined let no man sunder.*" In our affections let not St. Joseph be sundered from those, the best-beloved of God, to whom God has joined him so closely. May our Lord Jesus Christ give us more and more of that loving confidence towards St. Joseph, which burned so brightly in the hearts of St. Teresa, St. Francis of Sales, and so many glorious or hidden saints. And may St. Joseph, on his part, obtain for our cold and sinful hearts a little of that love for Jesus that filled to bursting his own most generous and magnificent heart, till at last it broke, and he died of love—love for the Sacred Heart.

THOUGHTS ON SAINT JOSEPH'S PATRONAGE

De quâcunque tribulatione clamaverint ad me, exaudiam eos, et ero protector eorum semper. " From whatsoever distress they shall cry to Me, I will hear them, and I will be their protector always."

These words, which occur in the thirty-sixth Psalm, are there applied to God as if spoken by God Himself; but the Church places them on the lips of St. Joseph in the Mass of the Feast of his Patronage. Many things that in their fulness are true only of God must in due measure be true of God's servants; and of His glorious servant St. Joseph *this* is true, that if any poor souls in distress cry out to him for help, he will hear them and will be their protector always.

Let us try at once to entitle ourselves to a share in the promise that St. Joseph thus makes to us all, by letting the following very simple and obvious considerations raise our hearts to him. Let us think of him and pray to him, and tell him how much we love

him ; and let us see if we may not learn to love and
honour him a little more.

For you and I, dear reader, are not in the least
afraid lest our love for God should grow cold according as our love for St. Joseph grows warm. Quite
the contrary. We know that any worth or beauty or
goodness that we can admire in St. Joseph, or in any
other creature, comes from God, and is less, when
compared with God's own incommunicable treasures
of beauty and goodness, infinitely less than one faint,
feeble ray of wintry twilight compared with the full
ocean of noonday sunshine that bathes a thousand
worlds in light and heat.

It is so plain to us children of the Catholic Church,
that honour paid to God's saints is honour and not
dishonour to God—our minds see this so clearly, and
our hearts feel it so strongly, that it seems an irritating
waste of time to discuss the point ever so slightly, as
if it could for a single moment be reasonably called in
question. Heresy forsooth pretends to be scandalised
at our praying to the saints, as if this were to ignore
God, to pass God by, to encroach upon God's rights.
Why, all that we do for the saints, we do for them
simply for God's sake, and because they are the dear
friends of God, and because He makes them His
proxies sometimes in doing us good and in receiving
our thanks. He delights in letting His poor children
do for Him and for each other what He could of

4

course, if He pleased, do without their aid. God is in this respect, as in many other respects, like a mother.

> " They bade me call Thee Father, Lord !
> Sweet was the freedom deemed ;
> And yet more like a mother's ways
> Thy quiet mercies seemed."

Will not a mother employ her children to carry her alms to the mendicant at her door, in order to train them betimes to almsgiving and to give them a share in her own merit? Nay, the unconscious infant at her breast—she takes a pleasure in making its little hand the medium of her bounty ; and if the poor mendicant looks gratefully on the smiling babe, and says " God bless you, dear !" is not this only a better form of thanks to the mother herself? So is it with our Father who is in heaven, and with His children who are in heaven or still on earth. These last are indeed needy mendicants—*Dei mendici sumus*, as St. Augustine says—while the Blessed are gathered, not into Abraham's bosom, but into the Heart of Jesus, into the Bosom of God. God does not always act immediately upon His creatures ; He employs their mutual services one for another. He could have pardoned Job's friends directly ; but no, He bade them first ask His servant Job to pray for them, as He desires us now to secure for ourselves the prayers of His saints in heaven.

And then from the creature's side—have we not enough of God in us, is there not sufficient generosity in our nature, to make us understand how a part of the heavenly joy and glory of the blessed may well consist in their being thus made the instruments of the Creator's goodness towards their fellow-creatures who are in exile and on their trial? Beatitude is not sleep or torpor or annihilation, but a blessed activity, perpetual life and vigour. And this is part of it. The desire which is felt by all good hearts on earth, the desire which Jesus Christ, who knows the human heart so well, attributes even to a lost soul in the parable (if it be merely a parable) of Dives and Lazarus—the desire of helping their brethren—how could the blessed saints of God fail to experience that desire, and how could our good God fail to gratify that desire by confiding to them, reigning with Him now in heaven, such a share in the salvation and sanctification of the Church Militant on earth as is implied in the beautiful and consoling doctrine and practice of the Invocation of Saints?

Among the saints whose intercession we are thus drawn to invoke, among these happy agents and instruments of the Divine goodness, one of the chief must necessarily be St. Joseph. The danger is not of going too far, but of not going far enough, when we say that there are few among the saints so useful in their example as he, and few so powerful in their patronage.

Yes, few so useful in their example; for the example set by St. Joseph can be copied by all of us at all times. We cannot all, except by generous desires, follow such saints as Francis Xavier to the ends of the earth, bearing the happy news of Christ to the nations that sit in darkness. We cannot all, like Thomas Aquinas, glorify God by devoting the grandest intellectual gifts to the illustration of the truths of faith. We cannot all scale the seraphic heights of love on which St. Francis of Assisi received the stigmas of Jesus. We cannot all of us, like Vincent de Paul, become the apostles of the poor and sick and suffering. But we *can* do what all these saints did also—we can study in the school of St. Joseph the virtues of the Hidden Life.

Humility, meekness, charity, love of work, love of prayer, persevering devotion to small daily duties: these are some of the lessons to be learned in the humble home of Nazareth. We all need such lessons. We have all in different vocations to live virtuous Christian lives, for the most part in obscurity and in a monotonous continuity of humble duties. St. Joseph's example teaches us the dignity of such a life, the great value of small things when done generously for God. The lowly carpenter did not work miracles, or practise great austerities, or preach to heathen nations. A holy and gifted man[1] asked quaintly enough: "What did Joseph do all his life but hammer nails with a pure intention? Yet Joseph is God's ideal of a saint."

One cannot have advanced far in the knowledge of the Heart of Jesus to be still in doubt as to the place which St. Joseph holds in that Heart. As he was nearest on earth, must he not in heaven be nearest and dearest to Mary and to Jesus? If God will not let a cup of water given in His Name go without its reward, what reward must He have given in return for the services that He deigned to accept from His Foster-father, the Spouse of His Blessed Mother—services that in their tender and continuous familiarity approach closest to the Divine Maternity itself. How great, then, must be the power of St. Joseph's Patronage!

St. Joseph is our Patron. In ancient Roman times persons of humble birth attached themselves as clients and dependents to some powerful nobleman who was their *patronus*, and who, as such, was bound to act towards them the part of adviser, guardian, defender. The saints in heaven are our patrons. Some are specially honoured and trusted by certain countries, as St. Patrick by Ireland—some by certain religious Orders which they founded or to which

---

[1] Father Tracy Clarke, S.J., Master of Novices in England about the middle of the nineteenth century, which is now practically over.

they belonged, as St. Francis of Assisi and St. Bona-
venture by the Franciscans, St. Dominick and St.
Thomas Aquinas by the Dominicans, St. Ignatius
and St. Francis Xavier and St. Aloysius by the
Society of Jesus—and others again are chosen by
individuals for the mere sake of their names or on
account of some personal attraction.   But the
Patronage of our great and glorious St. Joseph is
not monopolised by any class or any country.   He
is the Patron and the Protector of the Universal
Church, the Mystical Body of Christ, not only on
account of the relations which he held and holds to
Christ and His Mother, but because the Church has
solemnly installed him in this office, and bestowed
this title upon him, and because she had already
done so by establishing the Feast of St. Joseph's
Patronage.

The qualities of an efficient patron are power and
goodness—to be able and then to be willing to help
us.   St. Joseph has the power and the will.   His
power in heaven is in some sort the continuation of
his authority in the Holy Family on earth.   The
playful reasoning of the great Grecian warrior,
Themistocles, may with all reverence be applied
to our Saint.   "My little boy Astyages," argued
the Athenian leader, "is the real ruler of Greece:
for the infant's will is supreme with his mother,
and *she* rules *me*, and *I* rule Athens, and Athens

is the mistress of Greece." St. Joseph's prayer is more than a prayer when addressed to his Immaculate Spouse ; and she in turn exercises over her Divine Son the "suppliant omnipotence" of a mother.

Nay, we might venture to discover a parallel for St. Joseph's authority in another incident in the life of this Grecian hero. In one of the changes of his fate he had to fly from the anger of his people, and he took refuge in the palace of Admetus, King of the Molossi. Admetus was absent at the moment ; but his wife, pitying the illustrious fugitive, and knowing that her husband was hostile to him, advised Themistocles to take her child into his arms and sit as a suppliant at their hearth. The King Admetus soon entered his palace, and, seeing Themistocles thus, he took him under his protection and guarded him from his enemies. St. Joseph, too, was once a fugitive, but not for his own sake. "Arise and take the Child with His Mother." Nor was it for his own sake that the Mother of the Child bade him take the Child into his arms. It was to save that Child who was Himself a fugitive and in danger, although the Incarnate Son of the King of Heaven, our Lord and our God.

God never forgets, and the Heart of Jesus feels for Joseph at this moment the affection and gratitude that filled it when beating against St. Joseph's heart during the flight to Egypt. How great, then, is the power of St. Joseph's Patronage, equalled only by his fatherly tenderness and his eagerness to use that power in our behalf. May his holy Patronage help us to live, and help us to die!

THOUGHTS ON THE HIDDEN LIFE.

"How is it that you sought Me? Did you not know that I must be about My Father's business?" These questions recall to our minds a very remarkable and instructive passage in the life of our Divine Redeemer. That portion of the second chapter of St. John's Gospel tells us how our Lord and Saviour, Jesus Christ, when he was about twelve years of age, parted for three days from his Blessed Mother and St. Joseph, for this reason, amongst others, that He might show us that even the holiest human ties must yield to the higher, the supreme claims of God. Nothing whatever must stand in the way of God's will; nothing must hinder us from being about the business of our Heavenly Father. "Why is it that you sought Me? Did you not know that I must be about My Father's business?"

As a fact, these are the first recorded words of the Incarnate Word of God. He had spoken many words before this, and of course first of all to Her to whom also these words are addressed. The Babe of Bethlehem conformed Himself to all the pathetic feebleness of infancy. He made Himself like to us in everything except sin; and He was like to us in the gradual external development of His faculties, and, among the rest, of this most wondrous faculty of human speech. One might dwell in devout imagination on the earliest articulate syllables that may have been formed by the lips of the Child Jesus —His first words spoken no doubt to His Blessed Mother, like the first words of an ordinary Hebrew child or child of any other race. But all this is hidden from us. None of His words are preserved in the Sacred Scriptures till this conversation in the Temple; and it is with His Immaculate Mother that it is held. "Why is it that you sought Me? Did you not know that I must be about My Father's business?"

Simple words, yet strong with a Divine strength which has wrought many a prodigy since that day in the Temple when they first fell from the lips of our youthful Redeemer; words which ought to be often on our lips, and the spirit of them always in our hearts. In many a trial and temptation, in many an emergency small or great, these plain questions would overcome every difficulty and settle every perplexity. To evil thoughts, or to thoughts which, though not in themselves wrong, come to us at the wrong time, we may address the rebuke: "Why do you seek Me? Do you not know that I must be about My Father's business?" If bad companions whom we have given up, if dangerous occasions which we are trying to avoid, if amusement, wicked or foolish, which we have denied ourselves—if these or any other sources of temptation pursue us and find us out and complain of us for having deserted them, we are to repel them with the same Divine words: "Why do you seek Me? Do you not know that I must be about My Father's business?"

But, above all, this incident in the life of our Life is the typical tribute and homage to the supremacy of the Divine claims over all bonds of human affection, however pure and sacred. Never were human ties so sacred as those which bound, and which bind, our Lord Jesus Christ to His Blessed Mother; yet here He teaches us that all human ties, no matter how sacred, must give way to the one supreme obligation which binds the creature to the Creator, whose will alone is the sovereign, paramount, ultimate, and absolute end and aim of our being, of all that we do and say and suffer, and feel and think and are.

In particular, this question of our Lord, which we have already repeated so often, places the independent, absolute, and supreme rights of God sharply in contrast with the dependent, conditional, and subordinate rights which God has given to some of His creatures over certain of their fellow-creatures with whom He has linked their lots in various ways.

In our Lord's example here, the best reproof is administered to that idolatry of the domestic affections which pervades alike the world's most innocent romances and its grave treatises of morality. These all imply too often that the duties of creatures are limited to creatures, and that the end of man is nothing higher than man. Christ's answer to His Immaculate Mother is the best answer to the charges of heartlessness and cruelty brought against the Catholic doctrine of vocation—the heretical outcry against the whole system of religious life.

"Ah! your Saints have cruel hearts."

No, but it is your sinners that have the cruel hearts. The selfish worldling, the libertine, the sensualist, the gambler, the idle spendthrift, the drunkard—these have cruel hearts, starving often their little ones, sacrificing everything to self, breaking the hearts that have sacrificed everything for their sake. Nay, many who think themselves fond and devoted parents, render themselves liable to the reproach of selfishness and want of true feeling; while they who love not only well but wisely, who do not ignore the claims of God, but love those whom they love in God and for God, loving God above them all—these have the tenderest and truest and most loving of hearts, because their hearts are most like to the Heart of Jesus.

It is hard when a good father and mother look round, and, like Joseph and Mary, find the child of their love no longer in their company. Her place at home is vacant; they have lost her. But let them, like the parents of Jesus, seek her in the Temple. She has found Him whom her soul loves; Jesus has drawn her into His sanctuary, away from a world that was not worthy of her. And when a tender mother rebukes her meekly, " My child, why hast thou done so to us? "—she may indeed dwell on the security, the usefulness, the peacefulness, the quiet happiness, even as the days pass by, of the holy calling for which God in His goodness has given her sufficient aptitude and a strong inclination; and she may even contrast all this with the uncertainties, the sad possibilities, of other conditions which the world without a murmur would have allowed her to accept; but to the upbraidings and remonstrances of nature in her own heart, and in the hearts that she now loves better than ever, the answer of grace will still be the same question, the sternness of which the brave young novice may soften by a loving smile and an upward glance to Heaven: " Why did you seek Me? Did you not know that I must be about My Father's business? "

But let us go back to the actual scene in which these words were spoken first, and let us think a little more of the bearing of this question upon the conduct

of our Lord Himself. The Evangelist tells us in the
next sentence that, immediately after saying these
words, Jesus went down to Nazareth with Mary and
Joseph, and buried Himself again still deeper in the
Hidden Life from which He had for a day emerged—
hid Himself, not merely for another twelve years, but
for almost the entire term of His short mortal life
on earth.

What! Has He not this moment told us that He
must be about His Father's business? Yes; and
this *is* His Father's business. The work which the
Eternal Father had given Him to do was the salvation
and sanctification of the lost and sinful human race ;
and among the most potent means are the lessons
taught by the Hidden Life. These are practical
lessons which regard us all, for they help to make us
understand the greatness and holiness of such daily
homely duties as form the staple of our lives. St.
Paul tells us that every true Christian life is, as St.
Joseph's was in a more touchingly literal sense,
" hidden with Christ in God."

It was for this reason that our Lord spent so long
a time in teaching those lessons. If we were not
acquainted with the chief details of our Lord's life, but
only knew in general that He was to live on earth for
but thirty-three years in all; and if we knew, besides,
that this work was to convert the world through the
ministry principally of poor fishermen who were to be

slowly and painfully trained into apostles—if, with these facts only before us, we were asked to divide the years of our Lord's earthly pilgrimage between His private and His public life, we should be sure to assign to the latter all the years of his manhood. Yet His youth passed, and His maturity came, and still Jesus lingered on in the obscurity of Nazareth for eighteen years after He had asked the question: "Did you not know that I must be about My Father's business?" And all the years of His life before He put that question to Mary belonged likewise to His Hidden Life, nay, much also of what we call His Public Life, after He had in reality, not as at His first parting, parted at last from His Blessed Mother. Three hours were enough for His Agony upon the Cross, three days for all the mysteries of the Passion; three years, only three years, for the whole work of His Public Life—but ten times three years were given to teach us the lessons of the Hidden Life.

What are those lessons? The first lesson may be drawn from the very name by which we describe this portion of our Lord's career, calling it, as we have done so often already, His *Hidden* Life—a life hidden from the world, a life of lowliness and obscurity. Our Lord's example points to such a life as holy and blessed.

One part of God's creation often bears curious analogies to the other parts higher or lower; and one of these analogies is this—that of everything that is great much must be hidden. The spire that soars high into the air must rest on a strong foundation that sinks deep down beneath the surface of the earth. The ship with its huge tapering masts—how much of her is concealed under the sea over whose surface she seems to glide with such easy stateliness. And, as in material things, so also in things in which the spiritual nature comes into play. The man who would excel in any department of art and science—what a tedious apprenticeship of patient drudgery must first train his mind or his hand or his voice to the skill which seems in the end mere instinct or inspiration! The master of eloquent words has toiled long and painfully to acquire the perfect music that in the end flows almost spontaneously from his lips or his pen.

Nor is it in the beginnings only, or in the training and preparation. In every calling in life, in every position even the most eminent, and often in those highest places most of all, the soul has need of the strengthening, soothing, and purifying influences of the Hidden Life. Even worldly wisdom itself scorns and ridicules the weak natures who are fond of strutting before the gaze of the world, and who live on the breath of their poor fellow-creatures ; and a pagan, a very pagan writer, Sallust, sums up his praise of Cato by saying that he chose to be good rather than seem to be good, and that the more he fled from glory the more glory followed him.   One of the wisest of men, or at least one who has said the wisest things, makes one of his characters say—

> "I love the people,
> But do not like to stage me to their eyes.
> Though it do well, I do not relish well
> Their loud applause and *aves* vehement,
> Nor do I hold the man of safe discretion
> That doth affect it."[1]

And a famous statesman who flourished a little later than Shakespeare, Lord Clarendon, put over the door of his room in his place of concealment and exile in Jersey, in which, instead of fretting idly over his change of fortune, he employed his enforced leisure in writing the *History of his Own Time*, which has done most for his fame—*Bene vixit qui bene latuit*, "he has lived well who has lain well concealed."[2]

If this be the case, then, with regard to human and natural things, how much more in things supernatural and Divine.   *Ama nesciri* is the almost inspired counsel.   Believing in God and in our

---

[1] " Measure for Measure."—Act I. Scene i.

[2] Taken from the " Tristia " of Ovid :—

> " Crede mihi, bene qui latuit, bene vixit, et intra
>   Fortunam debet quisque manere suam."

> " He liveth well who loves his life to hide,
>   And each one ought within his lot to bide."

5

relations to God for time and eternity, the wonder is
that we have any difficulty in sinking down into the
hidden life of faith, in realising practically with St.
Francis of Assisi, that "what we are in the sight of
God, that we are and nothing more."

Ay, nothing more, and indeed nothing less also,
for this last point is almost as important as the other—
namely, our duty of recognising not only our worth-
lessness but our worth, not only our degradation but
our dignity. For God loves us. *Dilexit me.* The
wonder, as I said, is that we are allowed to think of
any other motive except this, to look to any eye but
God's. Yet it is of the Hidden Life itself that the
words are written : "And Jesus increased in wisdom
and age and grace with God and men."

But He was God, and in Him, even as man, the
fulness of wisdom abode : how could He increase in
wisdom ?   He increased, as the sun increases in
brightness from dawn to noon—the same sun, the
same light-giving substance, yet so different in the
effects of light and heat that it produces. The
Incarnate God, "the hidden God, the Saviour"
(Isa. xlv. 15) manifested more and more of His
Divine attributes as He advanced through the years
of His Hidden Life.

Like Him, we too must increase in wisdom and
grace, as in age. In age—ah yes, certainly, whether
we will or not ; and so, too, must we advance in

wisdom and grace, and this not only before God but before men.   Not before men only,—for God forbid we should be hypocrites,—our grace and wisdom must be true and real " before God who reads the heart, that God who seeth in secret may repay us."   Nor yet before God only, for God Himself, who forbids us to let our left hand know what our right hand does, orders us, nevertheless, to let our light shine before men.

A great deal might be said about the proper manner of reconciling precepts like these which seem to clash with one another, but which of course harmonise perfectly.   But we must hasten to an end, and there are two other characteristics of the Hidden Life besides its hiddenness, on which our minds must rest a little while before coming to an end.

Thus, in the second place, the Hidden Life of Jesus was a life of poverty and labour.   In the eighty-eighth Psalm, which refers prophetically to Christ, He is made to say, " I am poor and in labours from My youth."   Laborious poverty was His lot during His Hidden Life, which stretched far beyond His youth into His manhood ; and when He emerged from the Hidden Life, poverty and labour were with Him still. He had chosen poverty from the first, and He was consistent to the last.

But the poverty which God loves, the poverty of the first beatitude, the poverty of the Hidden Life, was

not the poverty of sloth or idleness, but the poverty
of hard and constant toil.   Some may, without any
fault of their own, be reduced to such a state of
untoiling poverty as is sometimes branded as pauperism, and we must not judge harshly even of those
who make mendicancy a trade; yet it is true that
God's blessing falls on poverty, not pauperism: it
does not fall on the poverty of drunkenness, and not
so much on the poverty of beggary or of the poorhouse,
as on the decent, high-spirited poverty of honest hard
work.

How poor must Jesus and Mary and Joseph have
been, and how hard they must have worked in the
Holy House of Nazareth!   Before that, what privations the Holy Family must have endured during
the exile in Egypt, depending for support on such
work and such payment as St. Joseph received from
strangers, the enemies of his race!   And after their
return they must still have fared very poorly, even
while our Blessed Lord helped St. Joseph at his trade.
That He did thus help him—that He was thus " poor
and in labours from His youth "—we are not left to
learn from tradition or from mere pious conjecture ;
for in St. Matthew's Gospel we read that, after our
Lord had begun His public life, the Jews said to one
another in surprise, " Is not this the carpenter's Son ? "
—and in St. Mark they ask more plainly still, " Is
not this the Carpenter, the Son of Mary? "   We may

imagine how rudely His employers often spoke in giving Him their orders for work ; we may imagine what privations their scanty and perhaps ill-paid wages left to be endured in Mary's household ; and in that modest household itself, besides the toils of the workshop, we may imagine all the humble services which the Son rendered to the Mother day by day.

When the devout mind sets itself to realise in devout contemplation what may have been and what must have been the actual everyday details of our Lord's Hidden Life, it is justified in drawing many necessary conclusions as to His outward demeanour and His internal feelings towards His Heavenly Father, and towards the two who shared with him the Holy Home of Nazareth. There is one feature, however, of the Redeemer's conduct during those secret years which the Holy Ghost will not allow us to overlook, inspiring the evangelists to condense the history of by far the largest part of Our Lord's life into the one brief phrase, *Erat subditus illis :* " He was subject to them." He, the Incarnate God of Wisdom and Power and Majesty, was subject to two of His creatures, the highest and purest indeed of all His creatures, yet still His mere creatures, infinitely beneath Him in dignity and power. Yet because Joseph was the shadow of the Eternal Father, He obeyed him ; and the Blessed Virgin Mary He obeyed as His own true and beloved Mother. What a useful lesson for us in all positions and degrees—a lesson more necessary perhaps than ever nowadays, when obedience and subordination and the gradations of society seem to be growing more and more irksome to men, and to need still more for their support supernatural motives and a Divine sanction.

Let us, then, study patiently and diligently in the school of Nazareth. Let us try to learn some of this humility and lowliness, this love of poverty and labour, —as far as our state of life calls for them or allows them,—this spirit of prayer, this obedience and charity, and all the other virtues of the Hidden Life. Jesus, "our hidden God, our Saviour," not only died for us ; He lived for us, and each incident of His life has its own lesson for us. Nothing happens by accident in any life, and least of all in this "life of our Life." The External Wisdom "ordered all things in it sweetly from end to end," from the crib to the cross —nay, earlier and later than crib and cross, from the womb of the Immaculate Virgin to the tomb hewn out of the virgin rock.

Our Divine Redeemer had special wise ends in view in coming amongst us precisely as He came. In fulfilling His eternal promise, "Behold, I come," He might have come in ways that would have dispensed with the Hidden Life. He might have come in full maturity, in all the power and majesty of perfect manhood transfigured by His Divinity. He might

have come as visible King of His own creation. He
might have come as a glorious and bloodless
Conqueror, some wondrous leader of men, more
eloquent than His poor creature Cicero, more intellectual than His poor creature Aristotle, more master-
ful than His far poorer creature Napoleon. He
might have come in the manifest plenitude of all the
mental and corporal gifts that are parcelled out
amongst the most gifted of the human race. Thus,
and in many other conceivable ways, He might have
come ; but He did not come thus. Ah ! if knowing
only the fact and the objects of His coming, we had
set ourselves to conjecture the circumstances that
might accompany it, never should we have been able
to guess the manner in which He actually came.
He came as the unborn and the newborn Child of
Mary, girded round with all those pathetic circumstances of poverty and feebleness on which pious
contemplation loves to ponder tenderly with adoring
awe ; and then He spent thirty years in the lowliness
and seeming inaction of the Hidden Life.

"Verily,"—to repeat for the last time the prophetic
exclamation of Isaiah—" verily thou art a hidden God,
a Saviour." Thou hast hidden Thyself, O Lord, under
many disguises in order to be our Saviour ; and we
must recognise Thee under all Thy disguises, and we
must imitate Thy Hidden Life if we would be saved.
If we would share in " the revelation of Christ's glory,"

those other words of St. Paul to the Colossians must be verified in us also: " You are dead, and your life is hidden with Christ in God "—even as Christ's own life, during the years which have here been brought before our minds, was hidden in God with St. Joseph and the Blessed Virgin Mary.

THE THREE JOSEPHS

THERE are more than three holy men bearing the name of Joseph, of whom mention is made in the Bible. Who, then, are the three whom we have grouped here together? The Foster-father of Jesus Christ our Lord is one of them, of course ; but who are the two other Josephs whom we honour by associating them with the Spouse of the Blessed Virgin Mary? There are three namesakes of St. Joseph mentioned in the genealogy of our Divine Redeemer which is given in the third chapter of St. Luke's Gospel : Joseph the son of Mattathias; and then, further back in the past, Joseph son of Juda ; and thirdly, much nearer to Abraham, or rather to Adam (for this retrograde genealogy reaches *him*), we have Joseph, not the son, but the father, of another Judas. Of these three Josephs, however, no facts are known that could be made the subject of a comparison between them and the Foster-father of our Lord. Joseph the Patriarch was not one of those three, for of the twelve sons of Jacob, not Joseph but Judas is named in St. Matthew's genealogy of our Lord. How often, by the way, that ill-omened name of the Traitor figures among the human ancestors of Jesus!

The first, then, of the namesakes and prototypes of our great St. Joseph, is Joseph son of Jacob and Rachel, of whom it is written in the thirty-seventh chapter of Genesis: "Now Israel loved Joseph above all his sons because he had him in his old age;" and of whom, too, it is written in the thirtieth chapter: "The Lord also remembering Rachel, heard her, and she bore a son, saying: God hath taken away my reproach; and she called his name Joseph." And it is also written of him by Ecclesiasticus (xlix. 17): "No man was born upon earth like Joseph, who was a man born prince of his brethren, the support of his family, the ruler of his brethren, the stay of the people."

It is true, indeed, that the brother of Benjamin is a type of our Divine Redeemer Himself, who was also hated by His brethren and was sold by them to His enemies, yet forgave them and saved them from destruction. But in one striking particular the two Josephs, who both were exiled into Egypt, resemble one another. Between the wicked wife of Putiphar and the Immaculate Virgin, between Zuleika and Mary, there is not resemblance but utter contrast; while the holy men to whom they were respectively entrusted are alike in the fidelity with which they fulfilled their trust.

Many other things that are narrated about the first Joseph are verified likewise in the last of the Hebrew Patriarchs and first of the Christian Saints. The King of Heaven has said to him, as Pharaoh said to Joseph: "Thou shalt be over my house" (Gen. xli. 40); and spiritual writers are fond of imagining that God bids us have recourse to the Patronage of the Spouse of Mary, by saying to us, as the King of Egypt said to his people: *Ite ad Joseph*—"Go to Joseph."

The other Joseph that deserves to be linked with him who has made the name so dear to us, is associated, not with the beginning, but with the ending, of our Lord's mortal life on earth. He is first mentioned in St. Matthew's Gospel, towards the end of the last chapter but one, and immediately after another Joseph who is named only in this place. After the centurion and others who had seen Jesus die had made their reluctant and faltering act of faith, "This indeed *was* the Son of God!"—we are reminded again of the more courageous faith proved by the women who had followed Jesus from Galilee, and who followed him to Calvary, "among whom" (we are told) "was Mary Magdalen, and Mary the mother of James and Joseph, and the mother of the sons of Zebedee."

This last was Salome, and the sons of Salome and Zebedee were St. John the Evangelist and St. James

the Greater ; whereas St. James the Less, the first
Bishop of Jerusalem, whose Epistle makes him the
Apostle of Extreme Unction, had for his brother
this other unknown Joseph, very dear, we may believe,
to our Lord, of whom he was so close a kinsman that,
according to the Hebrew way of speaking, he was
called the brother of Jesus.

After this mere naming of the Joseph who in God's
wisdom was left out of the plan of the Apostolic
College, not called with his brother James, as the
other James was called with his brother John, and as
Andrew was called with *his* brother Peter—after this
passing reference to the least known of the namesakes of our great Saint, for whose sake we have
named him, St. Joseph of Arimathea comes on the
scene, and plays so prominent a part there, that in
the sixty most devout and pathetic pages which
Father Gallwey in his *Watches of the Passion* devotes
to the "Taking down from the Cross," Joseph's
name is printed ninety-four times. No one can read
that holiest part of a very holy and beautiful book
without beginning to feel a special devotion to this
St. Joseph, gratitude towards him, confidence in him,
as a leader even among the saints of Calvary. A
man of wealth, a man of high social standing, he dares,
in that supreme moment when all are scared, to
risk everything ; and he goes boldly—*audacter*, as St.
Mark says—with a generous audacity, he goes to the

Roman Governor to ask for the Body of Jesus. He gains his object; the Sacred Body now belongs to Joseph, and is safe.

We are thinking of St. Joseph of Arimathea not for his own sake, but as representing, in a certain sense, the Foster-father of Jesus. Joseph's death of peace and honour had taken place before Christ's death of bitterness and shame; but what would have been his office here is confided to another who bears his name. To him, too, the Body of Jesus had belonged. It had been his privilege to protect and nourish the Child Jesus while He lay in His Mother's arms ; and now that He lies (but lifeless) in His Mother's arms again, it is the privilege of another Joseph to guard His sacred Body and provide a resting-place for it.

Another point of similarity between the beginning and the ending of our Saviour's life on earth, is the relation of type and figure that may be discovered between the Immaculate Womb wherein He lay at first, and then at the last the new sepulchre hewn out of the rock in which no man had yet been laid. With His last earthly dwelling St. Joseph of Arimathea provided Him. It was His last alms.

There is another link between Joseph of Nazareth and Joseph of Calvary. Like another Joseph, of whom we know nothing more with certainty— Joseph Barsabas, surnamed the Just, to whom Matthias was preferred to fill the place in the apostolic ranks left vacant by the treason of Judas—it is expressly stated of each of the two saints who presided respectively over the birth and over the burial of Jesus, " Joseph was a just man."   Now, as the Son of Man is just in a transcendent sense, and as it " behoves Him to fulfil all justice," what must be His recompense for the services He has deigned to accept at either extremity of His earthly career from these two glorious saints bearing the same beloved and oft-repeated name ?

But every type and figure and symbol falls short of the pathetic realities of the Divine Infancy.   No saint, except the Queen of Saints, has been allowed to approach so near to our Incarnate God, as the one great St. Joseph whose name has made us think of other Josephs.   He indeed it is whom the King of Heaven has placed over His household.   He indeed it is of whom the King of Heaven says to His people, *Ite ad Joseph.*   He indeed it is who kept guard over the Immaculate Mother and the Divine Child. " Whom God has joined let no one sunder ;" but let us in our hearts and in our prayers join together Jesus, Mary, and Joseph.   Let us beg of St. Joseph to plead for us with his Immaculate Spouse ; and let us beg of her to plead for us with her Son.   "And the King said to her : What wilt thou, Queen Esther ? What is thy request ?   If thou shouldst even ask one half of my kingdom, it shall be given to thee."   She craves now a smaller boon—only one poor heart, and this not for herself—but for Him, her Son. May it be given to her prayers that He may reign for ever in this poor human soul that wishes and prays to live and to die in His faith, in His fear, in His grace, and in His love.

AN IRISH PASTORAL ON SAINT JOSEPH[1]

ST. JOSEPH acted an important part in that scheme of redemption by which grace was purchased for us. It was Joseph who received into his arms the new-born Saviour ; it was he who watched over His infancy, with more than the affectionate solicitude of a parent; it was he who laboured with his own hands for His subsistence ; it was he, in fine, who, along with Mary, reared up the Victim destined for sacrifice. The Holy Ghost replenished the heart of this great Saint with an inconceivable tenderness of devotion to the Child of Benediction intrusted to his care—and who can tell the joys and griefs that mingled in that heart, as the sufferings and humiliations, or glories and triumphs, that awaited this thrice - beloved Child, presented themselves to his mind ? And now that he beholds, face to face, the Saviour whom he loved so devotedly on earth, now that the happy union with Him which commenced here below is perfected in heaven, who

[1] By the saintly and venerable Bishop of Ferns, Thomas Furlong, who was Professor of Theology at Maynooth College before being raised to the episcopacy. He died November 12, 1875.

can conceive the glowing ardours of that love, that fed
during life at the very fountain of Divine love, in the
cottage of Nazareth, and has now received its proportionate consummation in God's own tabernacles?
We may well rest satisfied, my dearly beloved people,
that our Saint harbours a similar tender affection
towards us who are the brethren of Christ, members
of the mystical body of which He is the Head.   Yes,
he is a father, a loving father to us all, as well as to
Jesus ; and if we fly to him for succour we shall soon
experience the effects of his fatherly love.   Let us
bear in mind, too, the surpassing dignity conferred
on Joseph here on earth.   God the Father shared
with him, as it were, His own paternity, and made His
own consubstantial Son subject to him.   How powerful, then, must his intercession be with Him who
acknowledged and bowed submissively to his authority
on earth !   Is it wonderful that a learned and pious
writer says that in heaven "St. Joseph does not
supplicate, but command "?

In all your trials and difficulties, therefore, go to
Joseph.   When the land of Egypt was afflicted of old
with a direful famine, the sovereign of that country
referred all his subjects who came to him for relief to
Joseph, whom he made governor over all his dominions.
Have you been visited with any temporal or spiritual
affliction?   Go to the minister of the great King, go
to Joseph.   It is he who, after Mary, has the largest

6

share in the distribution of the favours of Heaven. Are you poor and destitute, burdened with a numerous family looking to you for that nourishment which you cannot supply to them? Go to Joseph. He will find for you, in the granary of Divine Providence, aid and succour you little expected. Are you afflicted with a severe and tedious illness, and do you find your patience almost exhausted under this long and painful trial? Go to Joseph. His paternal heart will overflow with compassion for you, and he will obtain for you the restoration of health, or the patient resignation to the Divine will, which you desire. Parents, have you a child, the object of your fond solicitude, who, far from realising the fair promise of earlier years, has wandered away from the path of virtue and holiness he trod in happier days? Go, I repeat it, to the minister of the great King, and he will send forth His messengers, His heavenly graces, those harbingers of peace and reconciliation, that will invite the poor prodigal, nay, compel him, to return to his father's house. And, afflicted mother, have you a husband who, instead of being a fond partner to you, a kind father and guardian to his children, is the calamity and scandal of his household? Do you desire a powerful grace that will penetrate that obdurate heart and expel the demons that have taken possession of it? Fly to Joseph. Oh! the devoted Spouse of Mary, the fond guardian of the Infant God, will cast an eye of tenderest pity on you—he will ask, and not in vain, his own dear Jesus to impart to that hardened heart the devotion of conjugal affection and the tenderness of paternal love, to convert the outcast from heaven into a Christian, sober, industrious, and gentle ; to make your humble home, in some degree, represent the peace and purity of the cottage of Nazareth.

Unhappy sinner, are you overwhelmed by the consciousness of your own guilt, afraid to raise your eyes to Heaven to ask for mercy, and ready to sink into the abyss of despair? Go to Joseph—and he who, during his daily converse with the Redeemer of the world, learned so well "the length and breadth, and height and depth," of that charity that glowed in His breast, will become your mediator with Him ; compunction, love, confidence, will succeed to fear and despondency, and the peace of God, which seemed irrecoverably lost, will again cheer and gladden your heart. But above all, my dear people, by constant devotion to St. Joseph, engage him to become your guardian and protector at the hour of death. Ask him, who was so singularly blessed as to expire in the very bosom and embraces of his God, ask him, with his holy Spouse and her Divine Son, to be near you at that last awful hour, and to conduct you securely through the gates of death into the mansions of eternal bliss. In all your wants and necessities, therefore, have recourse to him whom

God has set over the treasury of His graces in
heaven, as He made him, on earth, the master of the
house that enshrined the fountain of all grace, the
Redeemer of the world. Offer up each day your
prayers to St. Joseph for the favours you stand in
need of, but offer them up with great earnestness,
and at the same time great confidence in his intercession. Bear in mind the remarkable words of St.
Teresa, the devout client of St. Joseph: " I never
remember to have asked anything of him which I did
not obtain." She at the same time addresses to all this
earnest request: " I shall now implore of all those who
may, perhaps, find it difficult to believe what I have
asserted, to make a trial of it themselves for the love
of God ; and their own experience will teach them
how advantageous it is to solicit the Patronage of the
glorious Patriarch." I earnestly entreat each one
amongst you, in offering up his supplications to
Heaven, through the intercession of St. Joseph, not
to forget the clergy and people of this diocese—to ask,
for the clergy, the Spirit of the Prince of Pastors
Himself, the spirit of humility and meekness, of
charity, self-sacrifice, and zeal, that, in the language
of the Church, " their doctrine may be the spiritual
medicine of the people of God, and the sweet odour
of their virtues may be the delight of the Church of
Christ ; " for the people, the spirit of obedience and
docility, of sobriety and temperance, the uncom-

promising faith, the unwavering hope, the generous charity, that warmed the breasts of their forefathers. Be, my dear brethren, assiduous and confiding clients of St. Joseph during life, and you will experience the benefit of his Patronage, especially at the critical moment of death.

AN ENGLISH TRIBUTE TO SAINT JOSEPH[1]

THE mysteries of St. Joseph rise up like a beautiful cloud of incense from the Sacred Infancy. He belongs wholly to it. It seems the one end for which he was created and so wonderfully sanctified, the one work which God gave him to do. He is altogether detached from the Passion. It does not even cast shadows over him beforehand as it does over the Mother of Sorrows. Nay, even before Jesus has left the Holy House for the toil of His Three Years' Ministry, Joseph has been taken to his rest. Worn out with divine love, he has died in a sweet ecstasy, pillowed on the bosom of Jesus, and, with Mary by his side, in the very lap of all that was most beautiful and most holy and most heavenly on earth. No thought of violence mingles with the memory of his peaceful though anxious offices. The Blood of the Circumcision was his Gethsemane and his Golgotha.

[1] Though we have here omitted many beautiful things from "The Foster-father and his Child," which is the fifth section of the second book of Father Faber's *Blessed Sacrament*, our extract is too long to be placed among the "Sayings of Holy Men about Saint Joseph," which will be given later.

His early life is lost in obscurity, and of his boyhood we can form no idea, beyond what is supplied by a vision of Sister Emmerich. But who can doubt that all was a preparation for the great office to which God had appointed him? Who can doubt that all was forming and consecrating him as the Foster-father of the Word made flesh? Belonging, as he does, exclusively to the Sacred Infancy, we shall not be surprised to find that the spirit of devotion to him is the spirit of devotion to the Sacred Infancy; and that with two additions of the most touching sort. First of all, he seems to represent ourselves in the Cave of Bethlehem, the Sojourn in Egypt, and the House of Nazareth. All the intimacy and familiarity to which the infant Saviour vouchsafes to give us right and title by His Incarnation, all the minute ministries of tenderness and devotion which He condescends to receive from us, all the daring joy which His infantine infirmities cause in our hearts, and all the trembling adoration which the nearness of His hidden Divinity demands from us,—all these things Joseph is there to receive and to pay, to feel and to show, as it were on our behalf. He is there as the representative of all the future generations of the faithful, especially of those whose hearts are drawn by a singular attraction to these first mysteries of Jesus.

But, secondly, St. Joseph is in Bethlehem, Egypt, the Wilderness, and Nazareth, as the shadow of the

Eternal Father. This is the immensity of his dignity. The incommunicable and ever-blessed Paternity of the Father is in figure communicated to him. He is the Foster-father of Jesus. To the world without he passes for His father. He exercises the authority of a father over Him, and performs for Him the affectionate and anxious offices of a father. Nay, in His human nature our Lord is subordinate to Joseph, whereas in His Divine nature He never could be subordinate to the Eternal Father. The unspeakable treasures of God, Jesus and Mary, are committed to St. Joseph's keeping, and he is himself a treasure, as well as the treasure-house of God. He is part of the scheme of redemption. Like Jesus and Mary, he has his types and forerunners and prophecies in the ancient covenant. He assists God in keeping the mystery of the Incarnation secret; and as the representative of the Eternal Father, he is to us, in his attendance upon the Holy Child, a perpetual memorial of His Divinity. By his very office, by that in heaven which he adumbrates, he reminds us at every turn that the Babe is Very God of Very God. Thus, while he teaches us the greatest familiarity, he also teaches us the greatest distance. While he encourages us to come near and kiss, he bids us also fall down upon our knees and adore profoundly the hidden Majesty of the new-born Eternal. Thus heaven and earth meet in him at Bethlehem, in his

double office of representative of the Eternal Father
and representative of faithful Christians. What
wonder theologians should tell us great things of
his copious graces and mighty gifts? What wonder
the faithful should believe[1] that with him the resurrection of the just had been anticipated, that he
was one of those who walked the streets of Jerusalem
at Easter in his risen body, and that he had borne
it with him into heaven, when he went up as part of
our Lord's equipage and retinue on the Thursday of
the Ascension?

What a gift it was which Jesus gave to His Church
in this tender and sublime devotion! Already had
the doctrine of our Blessed Lord been fixed and
ascertained. . . . The adoration of Jesus and the
devotion to Mary had taken their places immovably
in the sense of the faithful and in the practical
system of the Church, one shedding light upon the
other, and both instructing, illuminating, nourishing,
and sanctifying the people. But there was still one
more of the "earthly trinity," as it is called. Devotion to St. Joseph lay as it were dormant in the
Church. Not that there was anything new to be
known about him, or any fresh revelation to be made
of him. He belonged exclusively to the Sacred
Infancy. The beginning of St. Matthew's Gospel
contained him. By two evangelists he had been

[1] Suarez, *De Mysteriis.*

left in complete silence, and the third had barely named him in the genealogy. Tradition held some scanty notices of him, but they had no light but what they borrowed from St. Matthew. All we have known of St. Joseph was there then, only the sense of the faithful had not taken it up ; God's time was not yet come. The sense of the faithful was not like the complete science of the apostles ; it was not equal to it, it had to grow to it, to master it, to fill it out with devotions, to animate it with institutions, to submit to it as a perfectly administered hierarchy. But God's time came for this dear devotion, and it came, like all His gifts, when times were dark and calamities were rife. . . . Then it spread over the Church. Gerson was raised up to be its Doctor and theologian, and St. Teresa to be its Saint, and St. Francis of Sales to be its popular teacher and missioner. The houses of Carmel were like the Holy House of Nazareth to it, and the colleges of the Jesuits its peaceful sojourns in dark Egypt. The contemplative took it up and fed upon it ; the active laid hold of it, and nursed the sick and fed the hungry in its name. The working people fastened on it, for both the Saint and his devotion were of them. The young were drawn to it, and it made them pure ; the aged rested on it, for it made them peaceful. St. Sulpice took it, and it became the spirit of the Secular Clergy. And when the great Society of Jesus had taken refuge in the Sacred Heart, and the Fathers of the Sacred Heart were keeping their lamps burning, ready for the resurrection of the Society, devotion to St. Joseph was their stay and their consolation. So it gathered into itself Orders and congregations, high and low, young and old, ecclesiastical and lay, schools and confraternities, hospitals, orphanages, and penitentiaries, everywhere holding up Jesus, everywhere hand in hand with Mary, everywhere the refreshing shadow of the Eternal Father.—*Father F. W. Faber.*

SAYINGS OF SAINTS ABOUT
SAINT JOSEPH

JOSEPH is a paradise of delights.—*St. Ephrem.*

He gave to Joseph a father's love, a father's watchful care, a father's authority. — *St. John Damascene.*

By the name of father, no angel, no saint merited to be called ; Joseph alone could so be called.—*St. Basil.*

Some saints are privileged to extend to us their patronage in certain cases, but not in others, with peculiar efficacy ; but to our holy Patron, St. Joseph, it is given to assist us in all cases, in every necessity, in every undertaking.— *St. Thomas Aquinas,* IV. Sent. 9, 45.

Beyond all doubt Jesus in heaven not only does not refuse St. Joseph those marks of familiarity and reverence which He gave on earth as a son to a father, but He adds to them an increase. If you compare him to the whole Church of Christ, is he not the special and chosen being by whom and under whom the Lord was introduced into the world with becoming dignity ?   If all the faithful, then, are debtors to the Virgin Mother for being made worthy through her to receive the Redeemer ; so, next to that Virgin Mother, do we not owe to St. Joseph special homage and veneration ?—*St. Bernardine of Sienna.*

My beloved father and master, St. Joseph.—I took for my advocate and master the glorious St. Joseph, recommended myself much to him ; and up to this time I cannot remember having asked him for any-thing which he has not obtained for me. Would that I could persuade all men to prove by their own experience the advantage of devotion to this glorious Saint, and thus to receive their share of the blessings which he obtains from God ! I have never known anyone who was truly devout to him fail to advance rapidly in virtue ; for he assists in a most special manner those who recommend themselves specially to him. Oh that I could induce all to be devout to this glorious Saint, from the experience I have of his great power with God ! For many years past I have asked of him some favour on his Feast, which he never failed to obtain for me ; unless, perhaps, what I asked was not for my good. For the love of God, I implore those who do not believe me to make a trial of it, and they will soon find by experience how advantageous it is to have recourse to the glorious St. Joseph, and to become his devoted clients. It is wonderful what favours God has granted me by means of this blessed Saint ; from what dangers, both of body and soul, he has delivered me. God would seem to have given to other saints the grace to help us in some one necessity, but I have experienced that St. Joseph helps us in all, and that our Lord will have us understand that, as He was subject to Joseph on earth, so likewise in heaven the Saint obtains whatsoever he asks.—*St. Teresa, "Life,"* chap. vi.

Oh, what a saint is the glorious St. Joseph! He is not only a Patriarch, but the most distinguished among the Patriarchs. He is not merely a confessor, but far more than a confessor, for in him are included the dignity of the bishop, the generosity of the martyr, the excellence of the other saints. St. Joseph will obtain for us, if we repose confidence in him, an increase in every kind of virtue, but particularly in those which he possessed in a pre-eminent degree. These are a perfect purity of body and mind, humility, constancy, fortitude, and perseverance: virtues which will render us victorious over our enemies in this life, and enable us to obtain the grace of enjoying in the life to come those rewards which are prepared for the imitators of St. Joseph.— *St. Francis de Sales*, Entretien XIX.

Oh, how divine was the union between Our Lady and the glorious St. Joseph, a union which caused the Supreme Good, the Good of all goods, our Lord Himself, to belong to Joseph—even as He belonged to Our Lady—not by nature but by grace; which made him a sharer in all the possessions of his dear Spouse, and made him continually increase in perfection by his continual communications with her who possessed all virtues in so exalted a degree that no other creature, however pure and spotless, can attain to them! Nevertheless, St. Joseph was the one who made the nearest approach; and as a mirror when set before the rays of the sun reflects them perfectly, and another set before the first so vividly repeats them that it is scarcely possible to see which of the two immediately receives them, even so Our Lady, like a most pure mirror, received the rays of the Sun of Justice, which conveyed into her soul all virtues and perfections; and St. Joseph, like a second mirror, reflected them so perfectly, that he appeared to possess them in as sublime a degree as did the glorious Virgin herself.—*The Same.*

The example of Jesus Christ, who was pleased when on earth so to honour and to be obedient to St. Joseph, should alone be sufficient to inflame us all to be very devout to this great Saint. Suarez says that St. Joseph, next to Mary, surpasses all the other saints in merit and glory. We should particularly entertain devotion to St. Joseph, that he may obtain for us a happy death. In return for having delivered the Infant Jesus from the snares of Herod, he has the privilege of delivering the dying from the snares of the devil.—*St. Alphonsus.*

Let the evangelists be silent concerning all they could tell us of Joseph, placing in array before us those virtues and singular prerogatives which serve as a noble accompaniment to his dignity. To me it suffices that they make him known to us as the husband of Mary, that is, the most like among all living beings to the most perfect of pure creatures who ever came out of the hands of God, even His own Blessed Mother. Spouse of Mary! that is, who came nearest to that highest pinnacle of sanctity which pierced the heavens, which rose above the empyrean, and from the very bosom of the Eternal Father drew down His only-begotten Son. Spouse of Mary! that is, head of the first head in the world, for the husband is the head of the wife. Spouse of Mary! that is, lord of that sovereign Lady who well knew the precept of Genesis: "Thou shalt be under thy husband's power, and he shall have dominion over thee;" and who, most perfect in all else, was so also in the reverence and homage which she paid to her Spouse, in which reverence and homage she surpassed all other wives. Spouse of Mary! that is, of the great Queen, whom to serve is the highest dignity of the Dominations, the highest function of the Principalities, the deepest study of the Cherubim, and the most ardent desire of the Seraphim. "No more!" exclaims St. Bernard; "you say all in saying he was like the Virgin, his Spouse."

He was like her in all things: in countenance, in features, in heart, in disposition, in manners, in sanctity, in virtue; so that, if Mary was the aurora preceding the Divine Sun, Joseph was the horizon illuminated by its splendours.—*St. Leonard of Port Maurice.*

SAYINGS OF HOLY MEN ABOUT SAINT JOSEPH

THERE are other ministries appertaining to the order of the Hypostatic Union, which in its kind is more perfect, as we affirmed of the dignity of the Mother of God, and in this order is constituted the ministry of St. Joseph ; and although it be in the lowest grade of it, nevertheless in this respect it surpasses all others, because it exists in a superior order.—*Suarez.*

Since Joseph was to be the guardian, companion, and ruler of the Most Blessed Virgin and of the Child Jesus, is it possible to conceive that God could have made a mistake in the choice of him? or that He could have permitted him to be deficient in any respect? or could have failed to make him most perfect? The very idea would be the grossest of errors. When God selects anyone to perform some great work, He bestows upon him every virtue needful for its accomplishment.—*Bernardine de Bustis.*

The mysterious action of the Holy Spirit will not cease to move and inflame the hearts of the faithful, until the whole army of the Church Militant shall pay fresh homage to Joseph, raising monasteries, temples, and altars dedicated to his name. Yes, new and magnificent feasts will be celebrated in his honour, vows will be offered under his invocation, and those whose petitions have been granted will gladly fulfil them at his altar. God will give deeper penetration to human intellects ; and learned men, meditating on the interior and hidden gifts in Joseph, will be fain to acknowledge that no one ever possessed similar super-heavenly riches. Others are called the friends of Christ, but Joseph is called His father. The saints invoke Mary by the title of Queen, and this Queen is the Spouse of St. Joseph.—*Isidore Isolano, O.P.* (A.D. 1522).

Have I erred in saying that no one ever exceeded Joseph in sanctity, always, of course, excepting, as she ever must be excepted, his Spouse ? If such an assertion is to be esteemed temerity, then call Gerson, the famous Parisian Chancellor, temerarious ; temerarious a Bernardine de Bustis, a John of Carthagena, an Isidore surnamed Isolano, and, finally, a Suarez, whose judgment is equivalent to that of an entire university. And is it in ambiguous or obscure terms that Suarez expresses himself ? Listen to his words : " I do not see how it is a temerarious or improbable, but rather a pious and probable, opinion, should any hold that St. Joseph in grace and glory surpassed all the other saints, for there is nothing in Holy Scripture repugnant to such a belief."—*Segneri.*

Marvellous is thy sublime elevation, O Joseph! O incomparable dignity, that the Mother of God, the Queen of Heaven, the Sovereign Lady of the world, should not disdain to call thee her lord! Truly, truly, I know not which most to admire, the great humility of Mary, or the sublime grandeur of Joseph.—*Gerson.*

The Council of Constance approved the thought of Gerson, that St. Joseph should be the Protector of Christendom, and from that time the Church began to look upon the Holy Patriarch as her Universal Protector.—*Patrignani.*

He, as constituted head of the Family immediately belonging to the service of a God-Man, transcends in dignity all the other saints; wherefore he is happily established in an order which is superior to all the other orders in the Church.—*The Same.*

When Jesus came to cast fire upon earth, and desired that it should be enkindled, He chose some favoured souls in which He was sure to find it always burning. It found its expression in the "Magnificat," it made the Baptist leap for joy, it brought delight to the home of St. Zachary and St. Elizabeth, and shed a bright ray over the aged features of Simeon and Anna. Who can doubt, then, its power over the loyal and true heart of St. Joseph, and its daily and hourly increase, whilst in their journeys He was resting on that heart and was filling it with such feelings as St. John afterwards drew at the Last Supper from that inexhaustible spring of charity? . . . St. Joseph, above all, is the Patron and model of those who labour and are heavily burthened. He and our Divine Lord worked side by side for more than eighteen years, and were known to their neighbours only by the kind of work which was their only support. May our lives be guarded by St. Joseph's powerful intercession ; may he soothe us in sickness and cheer us in death, even as he himself sought and gained the only grace he desired to have—the grace of dying in the arms of Jesus and Mary.—*Dr. Thomas Grant, first Bishop of Southwark.*

It cannot be denied that in the first ages of the Church there appears a greater devotion to St. John the Baptist than to St. Joseph ; nowadays the very reverse is the fact. Why is this, if it be not because the worship of the Spouse of Mary and the father of Jesus is better suited to us than that of the mighty Saint who was the herald of His coming? There is no jealousy in heaven, and the great St. John, the very apostle of disinterested love, would willingly point to St. Joseph and say, as he did to our Lord, " He must increase, and I must decrease." The thought of the sweet Saint who guarded Jesus and Mary in their weary flight through the wilderness was to be more useful to Christians than the remembrance of the stern voice which sounded through the desert.—*Father Dalgairns, of the London Oratory.*

There were saints nearer to our Lord than either martyrs or apostles; but, as if these sacred persons were immersed and lost in the effulgence of His glory, and because they did not manifest themselves, when in the body, in external works separate from Him, it happened that for a long while they were less dwelt upon. As comparatively quiet times succeeded, the religious meditations of holy men and their secret intercourse with Heaven gradually exerted an influence out of doors, and permeated the Christian populace, by the instrumentality of preaching and by the ceremonial of the Church. Hence, at length, those luminous stars rose in the ecclesiastical heavens, which were of more august dignity than any which had preceded them, and which were late in rising for the very reason that they were so specially glorious. Those names, I say, which at first sight might have been expected to enter soon into the devotions of the faithful, with better reason might have been looked for at a later date, and actually were late in their coming. St. Joseph furnishes the most striking instance of this remark; here is the clearest of instances of the distinction between doctrine and devotion. Who, from his prerogatives and the testimony on which they come to us, had a greater claim to receive an early recognition among the faithful than he? A Saint of Scripture, the Foster-father of our Lord, he was an object of the universal and absolute faith of the Christian world from the first, yet the devotion to him is comparatively of late date. When once it began, men seemed surprised that it had not been thought of before; and now they hold him next to the Blessed Virgin in their religious affection and veneration.—*Cardinal Newman.*

For thirty years Christ lived with Mary and Joseph, and thus formed a shadow of the Heavenly Trinity on earth. O the perfection of that sympathy which existed between the three! Not a look of one but the other two understood, as expressed, better than if expressed in a thousand words; nay, more than understood — accepted, echoed, corroborated. It was like three instruments absolutely in tune, which all vibrate when one vibrates, and vibrate either one and the same note or in perfect harmony.—*The Same.*

Joseph was pure and innocent in a way unlike any other man who ever lived, our Lord excepted. His soul was white as snow. He had nothing whatever within his heart to make him ashamed, and he would have found it most difficult to find matter for confession. O Joseph, make me so blameless and irreproachable that I should not care though friends saw into my heart as perfectly as Jesus and Mary saw into thine. O gain me the grace of holy simplicity and affectionateness, so that I may love thee, Mary, and, above all, Jesus, as thou didst love Jesus and Mary. Joseph was as humble as he was sinless. He never thought of himself, but always of the Infant Saviour, whom he carried in his arms. O holy Joseph, make me like thee in purity, simplicity, innocence, and devotion. Jesus, Mary, Joseph, pray for me. —*The Same*.

What a beautiful death was St. Joseph's! Nursed in the arms of Jesus and Mary, his last hours were one long ecstasy. No anxious, no distressing thought was possible in that sweet company. For him death was only falling asleep to wake in Paradise. St. Joseph is therefore the Patron of a good death. Pray earnestly to Jesus, Mary, and Joseph, that you may die in peace in their blessed company.—*Father Richard Clarke, S.J.*

One of the great modern saints, to whom the Church owes the development of the devotion to St. Joseph, is St. Bernardine of Sienna. He was a great theologian as well as a great preacher, and a great saint and worker of miracles, and we have the advantage of possessing his sermons as revised by himself. They are, in truth, like those of Bour- daloue, very often complete theological treatises on the subjects with which they deal. In his famous sermon on St. Joseph, St. Bernardine lays down a great principle of the Kingdom of God as the foundation of his reasonings concerning the Saint. He says it is a general rule as to all singular graces which are communicated to any rational creature of God, that whenever the Divine favour chooses anyone for any singular grace or sublime state or position, He gives, with the vocation, those gifts of grace which are necessary for the person so chosen, and for the office to which he is chosen. He says that it is not only the graces absolutely necessary which are thus conferred, but those also which belong to the office by a kind of convenience, to embellish, and, as it were, decorate it duly and in fair proportion. This is the substance of the principle on which St. Bernardine insists. It is easy to see that this rule extends far beyond the occasion for which he uses it, which is the drawing out the graces which St. Joseph received as the Spouse and husband of Mary, and the reputed father of our Lord Himself. — *Henry James Coleridge, S.J.*

The theologians tell us that there is in the Kingdom of God an order still higher than that of the Apostolic commission, and this is the order of the carrying out the Hypostatic Union of the Human and the Divine natures in our Lord. Now it was in this order that the commission both of

Our Blessed Lady and of St. Joseph lay, and he was second in it to no one, except only to that Blessed Mother of God. His whole life and work in the Kingdom of God was spent in immediate contact with our Lord, and not simple contact merely, as might have been the lot of one who had lived with Him and been His constant companion for so many years, without having any special office in relation to Him. The office of St. Joseph could not be discharged without the most intimate and perpetual communication and companionship with Him and His Blessed Mother. He lived for our Lord and for her, he laboured for them, and watched over them, and guided and ruled them. It is in this, his participation in the order of the Hypostatic Union, that the saints see the reason for the foundation of the belief in his pre-eminent sanctity, in which, after the Mother of God, he has no compeer except in the blessed precursor, St. John, with whose name that of St. Joseph is coupled by the Church.— *The Same.*

In the writings of the ancient Fathers are to be found, not only what may be called prolific germs, but also positive and explicit statements of doctrine, which sufficiently show how deep in the consciousness of the Church lay the belief of Joseph's exalted dignity and sanctity, and how definite a shape it had assumed even in the early ages. The devotion paid to him has, it is true, been much more distinctly formulated in later centuries, when his place in the Celestial Hierarchy came to be more fully recognised ; but from the first this great Saint had a peculiar attraction for many holy and gifted souls, who regarded him with singular veneration and affection, as the citations given abundantly testify.— *Edward Healy Thompson.*[1]

Spend your life in honouring St. Joseph, and your love and homage will never equal the love and homage paid to him by Mary; it will approach never so distantly to the obedience, the love, the homage paid to him for thirty years on earth by the Son of God. But in proportion as your heart grows towards him in the reverence and unbounded confidence of a son, will you trace in your soul a more faithful copy of the Incarnate Word.—*Cardinal Vaughan.*

How can we sufficiently admire the unremitting, uncomplaining, self-sacrificing toil of Joseph, who was honoured by the Eternal Father with the office of governing and working for His Eternal Son and the Ever-Blessed Virgin Mother! How shall we wonder at the sweet, gentle, assiduous labours of Mary, watch-

---

[1] We are glad to quote this devout layman, whose *Life and Glories of St. Joseph, Husband of Mary, Foster-father of Jesus, and Patron of the Universal Church*, is one of the finest and most complete treatises on this Holy Patriarch that any literature possesses.

ing over the comfort of her husband and her Child, never forgetting nor omitting anything which might cheer or alleviate their earthly lot, and brightening their home with her beautiful and loving smiles. How shall we adore the gracious Child, advancing daily in wisdom and age, and grace with God and man ; manifesting ever more and more to His parents' wondering eyes the hidden perfections of His God-head, and captivating their love by His reverent obedience and sweet attentions and gentle loving ways. What a school of love was there ! Jesus the Ocean of created love and charity ; Mary full of grace and love as much as was possible to a pure creature ; Joseph, the Guardian-Father of Jesus, the Virgin-Husband of Mary, the Companion and Disciple of both, and filled by God with that supreme love which such offices required. Every kind of created tenderness was there, following upon charity, and unspeakably dear to the God of charity, who has known how to create so many varieties and sweet-nesses of love in the heart of man. There was the ineffable mutual love of husband for wife, and of wife for husband, intensified as well as purified by the virginity of both. There was the love of father and the love of mother for their Child ; for He was the Child of both, pre-ordained to be the recompense and bond of their virginal union. There was the love of the Child for His parents, intense and perfect, as must have been every kind of love in the Sacred Heart of God.—*Edward Bagshawe, Bishop of Nottingham* (A.D. 1887).

I have seen a little picture which represents St. Joseph with the Divine Infant, who points towards him, saying : *Ite ad Joseph!* To you I say the same, Go to Joseph ! Have recourse with special confidence to St. Joseph, for his protection is most powerful, now above all that he is the Patron of the Universal Church.—*Pius IX.*

Why St. Joseph should be regarded specially as the Patron of the Church, and why the Church in turn should promise much to herself from his guardianship and patronage, these are the decisive causes and reasons : that he is the husband of Mary and the putative father of Jesus Christ. From this have proceeded all his dignity, grace, sanctity, and glory. Certainly the dignity of Mother of God is so exalted that nothing greater can be made ; but nevertheless, because there existed between Joseph and most Blessed Mary the bond of marriage, it is beyond all doubt that he approached nearer than any other to that most excellent dignity by which the Mother of God far surpasses all created natures.—*Leo XIII.*

A FEW PRAYERS TO SAINT JOSEPH

———◆———

THIRTY DAYS' PRAYER TO SAINT JOSEPH

IN HONOUR OF THE THIRTY YEARS SPENT WITH JESUS AND MARY

To be offered for any special intention.

EVER blessed and glorious Joseph, kind and indulgent father, and compassionate friend of all in sorrow! through that bitter grief with which thy heart was saturated when thou didst behold the sufferings of the Infant Saviour, and in prophetic view didst contemplate His most ignominious Passion and Death, take pity, I beseech thee, on my poverty and necessities, counsel me in my doubts, and console me in all my anxieties. Thou art the good father and protector of orphans, the advocate of the defenceless, the Patron of those who are in need and desolation. Do not then disregard the petition of thy poor child. My sins have drawn down upon me the just displeasure of my God, and hence I am surrounded with sorrows.

To thee, O loving guardian of the poor neglected Family of Nazareth, do I fly for shelter and protection.

Listen, then, I entreat of thee, with a father's solicitude, to the earnest prayer of thy poor supplicant, and obtain for me the object of my petition. I ask it by that infinite mercy of the eternal Son of God, which induced Him to assume our nature, and to be born into this world of sorrow. I ask it by that grief which filled thy heart, when, ignorant of the mystery wrought in thy Immaculate Spouse, thou didst fear thou shouldst be separated from her.

I ask it by that weariness, solicitude, and suffering which thou didst endure when thou soughtest in vain at the inn of Bethlehem a shelter for the Holy Virgin, and a birthplace for the Infant God, and when, being everywhere refused, thou wert obliged to consent that the Queen of Heaven should give birth to the world's Redeemer in a wretched stable.

I ask it by the painful blood-shedding thou didst witness at His circumcision. I ask it by the sweetness and power of that sacred name, JESUS, which thou didst confer on the adorable Infant. I ask it by that mortal anguish inflicted on thee, by the prophecy of holy Simeon, which declared the Child Jesus and His Holy Mother to be the future victims of their own great love for us and of our sins. I ask it through that sorrow and anguish which filled thy soul, when the angel declared to thee that the life of the Child

Jesus was sought by His enemies, from whose impious design thou wert obliged to fly with Him and His Blessed Mother into Egypt.

I ask it by all the pains, fatigues, and toils of that long and perilous journey. I ask it by all the sorrows thou didst endure when in Egypt, when sometimes thou wert not able, even by the sweat of thy brow, to procure daily food for thy poor Family.

I ask it by all thy solicitude to preserve the Sacred Child and His Immaculate Mother, during thy second journey, when thou wert ordered to return to thy native country. I ask it by thy peaceful dwelling in Nazareth, in which so many joys and sorrows were mingled. I ask it by thy extreme affliction, in being three days deprived of the company of the adorable Child. I ask it by thy joy at finding Him in the Temple, and by the unspeakable consolation imparted to thee in the cottage of Nazareth, while living in the society of the Infant Jesus. I ask it by that wonderful condescension by which He subjected Himself to thy will.

I ask it through that sorrowful foresight thou hadst continually in thy mind, of all the Infant Jesus was to suffer, when thou shouldst be no longer by His side.

I ask it by that painful contemplation, by which thou foresawest those Divine Infant Hands and Feet, now so active in serving thee, one day pierced with cruel nails; that Head, which rested gently on thy breast, crowned with sharp thorns; that delicate Body, which thou didst tenderly fold in thy mantle and press to thy heart, stripped, mangled, and extended on a cross.

I ask it by that heroic sacrifice of thy will and best affections, by which thou didst offer up, years beforehand, to the Eternal Father the last awful moment, when the Man-God was to expire for our salvation.

I ask it by that perfect love and conformity with which thou didst receive the Divine order to depart from this life, and from the company of Jesus and Mary. I ask it by that exceeding great joy which filled thy soul when the Redeemer of the world, triumphant over death and hell, entered into the possession of His kingdom, and conducted thee also into it with especial honours. I ask it through Mary's glorious Assumption, and through that endless bliss, which, with her, thou wilt eternally derive from the presence of God.

O good father! I beseech thee, by all thy sufferings, sorrows, and joys, hear me, and obtain the grant of my earnest petitions. [*Here name them or reflect on them.*] Obtain for all those who have asked my prayers, all that is useful to them in the designs of God. And finally, my dear Patron and Father, be thou with me and all who are dear to me, in our last moments, that we may eternally chaunt the praises of Jesus, Mary, and Joseph in Heaven.

8

VENERABLE OLIER'S SALUTATIONS TO SAINT JOSEPH

HAIL, Joseph, image of God the Father!

Hail, Joseph, Foster-father of God the Son!

Hail, Joseph, treasury of the Holy Spirit!

Hail, Joseph, delight of the Blessed Trinity!

Hail, Joseph, most faithful coadjutor of the Incarnation!

Hail, Joseph, most worthy spouse of the Virgin Mary!

Hail, Joseph, father of all the faithful!

Hail, Joseph, guardian of holy virgins!

Hail, Joseph, greatest lover of poverty!

Hail, Joseph, example of meekness and patience!

Hail, Joseph, mirror of humility and obedience!

Blessed art thou above all men:

And blessed be thy eyes which have seen the things which thou hast seen;

And blessed be thy ears, which have heard the things which thou hast heard;

And blessed be thy hands, which have touched and handled the Incarnate Word;

And blessed be thy arms, which have carried Him who carries all things;

And blessed be thy breast, on which the Son of God most sweetly rested;

And blessed be thy heart, inflamed with burning love:

And BLESSED be the ETERNAL FATHER, who chose
    thee ;

And BLESSED be the SON, who loved thee ;

And BLESSED be the HOLY SPIRIT, who sanctified
    thee ;

And blessed be thy Spouse, Mary, who loved thee as
    a Spouse and a brother ;

And blessed be the angel who watched over thee ;

And blessed be for ever all who bless and love thee.

Amen.

PRAYER TO SAINT JOSEPH

WE turn in our trouble to thee, Blessed Joseph,
and after praying for aid from thy Holy Spouse, we
seek with confidence thy Patronage also. By the
affection that united thee to the Virgin Immaculate,
Mother of God; by the fatherly love wherewith thou
didst surround the Infant Jesus ; we beseech thee to
help us to the possession of the heritage that Jesus
Christ conquered for us by His Blood, and to aid us
by thy power and succour in our need.

Foster, O thou most wise guardian of the Holy
Family, the elect people of Jesus Christ. Keep us,
O thou most loving father, from every stain of error
and corruption. Be favourable and help us from the
heights of heaven, O thou our most mighty deliverer,
in the fight we must wage against the powers of

darkness. And even as thou didst once snatch the Child Jesus from the danger of death, so now defend the Holy Church of God from the snares of the enemy and from all adversity. Grant us thy perpetual protection, so that, sustained by thy example and thy help, we may live in holiness, and die in piety, and reach the everlasting blessedness of Heaven. Amen.

ACT OF CONSECRATION TO SAINT JOSEPH

BY THE VENERABLE HENRI BOUDON

I CAST myself down in your holy presence, O glorious St. Joseph, and I honour you as the chaste Spouse of the Mother of God, head of the Holy Family, Foster-father of our Lord Jesus Christ, and guardian of the treasures of the most Holy Trinity. I revere in you the choice of God the Father, who wished to share with you His authority over His Divine Son; the choice of God the Son, who wished to be dependent on you, and to owe His support to the labour of your hands; the choice of God the Holy Ghost, who wished to confide to you His Immaculate Spouse, and to give her to you as your companion. I congratulate you on your happiness in carrying Jesus in your arms, pressing Him to your breast, embracing Him lovingly, and weeping over Him with joy during the holy caresses with which you were so often favoured by this Divine Child. Who could comprehend the treasures of light and grace and wisdom with which your soul was enriched during the thirty years which you spent with Jesus and Mary?

Penetrated with reverence and love at the sight of your greatness and holiness, I consecrate to you my heart. Henceforth I will look on you as my father and protector; deign to look on me as your child. Make me feel the effects of your great power with God, and of your great charity towards me. Obtain for me the grace of true conversion, and all the graces I need to accomplish God's adorable designs. Obtain for me that spirit of recollection, that interior life, that fidelity to grace, that intimate union with God, that profound humility of heart, that perfect conformity to God's pure and holy will, that patience in trials, that love of the Cross, that perfect abandonment of self to the guidance of Divine Providence, above all, that ardent love for Jesus Christ and for His Blessed Mother, for which you were pre-eminently distinguished. O great Saint, take all interior souls under your protection, those especially who, after your example, hear and imitate Jesus and Mary in silence and retirement. In fine, by your privilege of dying most happily in the arms of Jesus and Mary, obtain for me, O great Saint, a death like to yours in the perfect conformity of my will with the will of Jesus and of Mary. Amen.

ANOTHER ACT OF CONSECRATION TO SAINT JOSEPH

GREAT St. Joseph, most chaste Spouse of the Queen of Virgins, Foster-father of the Word made flesh, I choose thee to-day as my special protector against all my enemies. I pledge myself to remain faithful to thee till death, and to advance thy honour as far as it may be in my power. In return, O great Saint, deign to admit me into the number of thy clients, enlighten me in my doubts, strengthen me in my feebleness, comfort me in my sorrows, protect me in my last hour, and help to bring me safe to heaven, there to praise with thee for ever the most holy and adorable Trinity. Amen.

INDULGENCED ASPIRATION TO SAINT JOSEPH

GLORIOUS St. Joseph, deign to pray for us and for the Souls in Purgatory.

(*One hundred days' Indulgence*—LEO XIII., April 13th, 1888.)

THE MEMORARE OF SAINT JOSEPH

REMEMBER, O most illustrious and glorious Patriarch St. Joseph, that, according to the testimony of St. Teresa, your devoted client, it is unheard of that anyone ever had recourse to your protection, implored your assistance, or sought your mediation, without obtaining relief. Confiding, therefore, in your goodness, my most loving father, chaste Spouse of Mary, behold me prostrate in spirit at your feet, humbly begging of you, O just Joseph, Foster-father of Jesus, and dispenser of the treasures of His Sacred Heart, not to despise my earnest prayer, but graciously to hear and obtain for me the grant of my petitions. Amen.

(*Indulgence three hundred days ; applicable to the Souls in Purgatory*, June 26th, 1863.)

INDULGENCED PRAYER TO SAINT JOSEPH

For Priests before Mass.

Oh, how happy was St. Joseph, to whom it was given to see and hear God, whom many kings desired to see and saw not, desired to hear and heard not! Nay, to whom it was granted not only to see and hear Him, but to carry, to kiss, to clothe, and to guard Him.

℣. Pray for us, Blessed Joseph,

℟. That we may be made worthy of the promises of Christ.

Let us pray.

O God, who hast given to us a royal priesthood, grant, we beseech Thee, that as St. Joseph merited to touch reverently with his hands and to carry in his arms Thy only-begotten Son, who was born of the Virgin Mary, so mayest Thou make us minister at Thy holy altars with cleanness of heart and innocence of conduct, in order that we may to-day receive worthily the sacred Body and Blood of Thy Son, and may merit to have an eternal reward in the world to come. Through Christ our Lord. Amen.

THE UNFAILING PETITION

HOLY St. Joseph, Spouse of Mary, be mindful of me, pray for me, watch over me. Guardian of the Paradise of the New Adam, provide for my temporal wants. Faithful guardian of the most precious of all treasures, bring this matter that concerns me to a happy end, if it be to the glory of God and the good of my soul. Amen.

MOST EFFICACIOUS PRAYER TO SAINT JOSEPH

O GLORIOUS St. Joseph! faithful follower of Jesus Christ, to thee do we raise our hearts and hands to implore thy powerful intercession in obtaining from the benign Heart of Jesus all the helps and graces necessary for our spiritual and temporal welfare, particularly the grace of a happy death and the special favour we now implore [*mention it*].

Glorious St. Joseph, we feel animated with

confidence that thy prayers in our behalf will be graciously heard before the throne of God.

[Then say the following Versicle and Response seven times in honour of the seven joys and sorrows of St. Joseph.]

℣. O Glorious St. Joseph, through the love thou bearest to Jesus Christ and for the glory of His name,

℟. Hear our prayers and obtain our petitions.

A SHORT PRAYER TO SAINT JOSEPH

O DEAR St. Joseph, Foster-father of our Divine Redeemer, and Spouse of our Holy Mother Mary! You lived with them and toiled for them through all the years of the Hidden Life, and you died in their arms. By the love you bear to them, and the love they bear to you, pray for us always, and guard us. Obtain for us, O Patron of a happy death! the grace to live and die in God's love and favour, that we may spend our eternity with Jesus and Mary and with you, O dear St. Joseph.　　　M. R.

SAINT JOSEPH'S AFTERMATH

Supplement to " Saint Joseph's Anthology "

———◆———

SPOUSE DIVINE AND HUMAN

My Lady, yea, the Lady of my Lord,
Who didst the first descry
The burning secret of virginity,
We know with what reward ;
Prism, whereby
Alone we see
Heaven's light in its triplicity ;
Rainbow complex
In bright distinction of all beams of sex,
Shining for aye
In the simultaneous sky,
To One, thy Husband, Father, Son, and Brother,
Spouse blissful, Daughter, Sister, milk-sweet Mother,
" Ora pro me."

Mildness, whom God obeys, obeying thyself
Him in thy joyful Saint, nigh lost to sight

In the great gulf
Of his own glory, and thy neighbour light;
With whom thou wast as else with husband none,
For perfect fruit of inmost amity;
Who felt for thee
Such rapture of refusal, that no kiss
Ever sealed wedlock so conjoint with bliss;
And whose good singular eternally
'Tis now, with nameless peace and vehemence
To enjoy thy married smile,
That mystery of innocence,
" Ora pro me."

COVENTRY PATMORE.

ITE AD JOSEPH

A LEGEND

BETWEEN the soul and the Blessèd Land
St. Peter stood, with the Keys in his hand—

" Thou hast lived in sin, and hast died in sin,
And thou mayest not enter the Gate within."

But the poor soul cried only, " St. Joseph, attend!"
Cried ever, " St. Joseph! my father, my friend,

" They say I have sinned—and it well may be—
But was not I always devout to thee?

" Did ever my feet through a church-door go,
But before thine image I louted low?

"Chapel of thine have I ever sought,
But I lighted candle, or roses brought?

" Have not I cleaved to thee, sick and well?
And wilt thou permit me to fall into Hell?"

Faithful father, St. Joseph came;
But ever St. Peter spake the same:

" He has died in sin, and sin that was great,
And now shall he enter within the Gate?"

To the Angel Choir, whose wings seemed dipped
In sunset glory, and glory-tipped,

St. Joseph ran, and on to the Choir
With wings like a harvest field on fire;

The First fair Order hushed, when they heard,
Their citherns, and hushed them the Second and
    Third,

Till, each after each, had gone Orders eight,
And the Ninth Order last of all, down to the Gate,

And left not aught they could say unsaid;
But ever St. Peter shook his head.

Through golden street upon golden street,
Went St. Joseph with hurrying feet,

Till one by one, and by twos and threes,
The Saints came down 'neath the blossoming trees,

Saint after Saint down the lilied stair,
Till all the Blessèd in Heaven were there ;

But ever his head St. Peter shook,
And ever his way St. Joseph took

Past the meadows, where never a soul
Remained, nor an Angel played cithole ;

Farther yet through the Blessèd Land,
To one that was seated at Christ's Right Hand.

In her pearly vesture, and mantle spun,
And from dew-bright rays of the morning sun ;

More fair than the twelve white stars in her crown,
The Mother of God to the Gate came down.

The angels at sight of her struck the strings,
Till the sound ran to meet her, like rushing of wings,

All of silver.   St. Peter that held the Keys,
Unmitred before her and went on his knees.

Ringed round her the Saints, like aureole clear,
But "Yea" from St. Peter none could hear.

Then, ever in haste, St. Joseph ran
To Him who, when scarce He measured a span,

Had lain in St. Joseph's arms and smiled,
And clung to his neck, a two years' child ;

With the strange buried flowers, as it were, shining
      sweet,
Shining large through His hands, through His side,
      through His feet,

In a mist of glory and golden state,
Mary's Son went down to the Gate ;

And God Almighty looked from His throne,
And saw He was left in Heaven alone.

At His will returning, a soft white flame
Dividing the silence, a seraph came,

And told how all Heaven, from south and from
      north,
At St. Joseph's prayer had in turn gone forth ;

And, for sake of St. Joseph, were gathered a great
Multitude beautiful down at the Gate.

Spoke God our Lord—and His smile was kind—
" Go, say that St. Peter must change his mind.

" Without court, without singers, am I to stay
Till what time St. Joseph has got his way ?

" If St. Joseph's prayers are to empty Heaven,
Go, say that his client must be forgiven." [1]

MAY PROBYN.

SAINT JOSEPH'S SECRETS

SAINT JOSEPH, did He croon like some sweet dove
    At thy approach and at thy smiling beck ?
And didst thou clasp th' Incarnate God of Love,
    And were His baby arms flung round thy neck ?

And didst thou watch Him grow from age to age—
    The babe forgotten in dear childhood's time,
The child but half-remembered at the stage
    Of boyhood's growth and through its rosy prime ?

And didst thou marvel at His upturned face,
    His shining eyes—soft pools of heavenly light ?
Was not each gesture clothed with winning grace,
    A holy picture to thy saintly sight ?

[1] This playfully extravagant hyperbole of confidence in St. Joseph's intercession is sometimes expressed still more naïvely and less poetically ; and some have thought fit to be a little scandalised at it. But the Spaniards have a saying to the effect that you cannot have a full and firm faith till you are able to jest lovingly about the objects of your faith ; and the simplest Spanish peasant would be able to season such a legend as this with the proper allowance of salt.—THE EDITOR.

And did He speak in boyhood's silver speech,
    And was thy hearing by His treble thrilled?
As ever David's hymns thine ears would reach,
    Was not the workshop by His singing filled?

And did He wait on thee and do thy will,
    Wield saw and hammer fore and after noon,
Bending to labour till the twilight chill
    Led to a needed rest as rose the moon?

And was the night-long silence very deep?
    And did child-angels crowd about His bed
To worship as He lay in placid sleep,
    And make a glory round His royal head?

Was not the morning music of His prayer
    The sound that greeted first thy waking sense?
Was not the smile upon His features fair
    Brighter than dawn in all its radiance?

Oh, surely day began in peace and bliss,
    And toil was sweeter far than night's own rest;
For He would meet thee with a son's own kiss,
    And thou wouldst bless Him—GOD for ever blest.

And, after those Three Days of dolorous loss,
    Did He one eve His destiny impart,
That awful secret of the coming Cross?
    Was this the death-wound of thy loving heart?

Or didst thou die in happy ignorance
    Of all the agony and bitter pain,

The scourging and the thorns, the nails and lance,
   Endured by GOD'S dear Lamb without a stain?

All these, St. Joseph, these—and how much more!
   All these and countless joys some day thou'lt tell,
When we thy clients gather on the shore
   Of God's great Sea of Love ineffable.

DAVID BEARNE, S.J.

TO SAINT JOSEPH

A ROUNDEL

CHASTE Spouse of her, the Mother of God's Son,
   And servant of the Blessèd Trinity!
In that far Heaven, where thou a crown hast won,
   St. Joseph, pray for mine, and pray for me.

Like all of us, thou hast thy sorrows known,
   When thou on earth wert by God's high decree
Chaste Spouse of her, the Mother of God's Son,
   And servant of the Blessèd Trinity!

And surely He who in the days long flown
   Ate of thy bread and rested on thy knee,
When Egypt's idols in the dust lay prone,
   In His own home will nought deny to thee,
Chaste Spouse of her, the Mother of God's Son,
   And servant of the Blessèd Trinity!

MAGDALEN ROCK.

9

SAINT JOSEPH

FOREMOST amid the glorious throng,
    From every age and clime,
Praising their God with bursts of song
    And heavenly strains sublime;
'Mid martyrs blest and virgins pure,
    With brighter diadem
Reigns he, the poor, despised, obscure
    Toiler of Bethlehem.

And it is meet that he should bear
    The lily in his hand,
Should crown of dazzling lustre wear,
    Should nigh the Godhead stand.
For he, of all men born, alone
    Was worthy deemed to be
Spouse of the one who nursed the Son
    Of God upon her knee.

And if on earth all lowly he,
    If men knew nought of him,
Sublime his place in Heaven must be
    Above the Cherubim;
For He who sits upon God's right,
    Who our salvation won—
When day was night on Calvary's height,
    Was Joseph's Foster-Son.

And blest are we a thousand fold,
    E'en in our direst need,
If to the Babe he saved of old
    Joseph for us will plead !
Oh, blest a thousand fold are we
    Beneath St. Joseph's care,
For Mary shares in Joseph's prayers
    And Jesus grants their prayer.

                       MAGDALEN ROCK.

LOTUS AND LILY

SOMETIMES a dark hour cometh for us who are
    bound to bear
The burden of lowly labour, the fetters of lowly care.

An hour when the heart grows sick of the work-day's
    weary round,
Loathing each oft-seen sight, loathing each oft-heard
    sound !

Loathing our very life, with its pitiful daily need,
Learning in pain and weakness that labour is doom
    indeed.

And this the need of the struggle—tent, and raiment,
    and bread ?
Oh for the " Requiescant," and the sleep of the
    pardoned dead !

Oh, the visions that torture and tempt us (how shall
    the heart withstand?)—
The fountains and groves and grottoes of the God-
    less Lotus-land!

Oh, the soft, entreating voices, making the tired
    heart leap:
"Come over to us, ye toilers, and we will sing ye to
    sleep."

A fatal sleep, I trow! but we are sad unto
    death,
And the Lotus flower unmans us with its sweet and
    baneful breath.

We look to our fellow-toilers — what help, what
    comfort there?
They're bowed by the self-same burden, beset by the
    self-same snare.

Falleth the ashen twilight, meet close for the dreary
    day;
Hark to the chimes from the church-tower—but we
    are too tired to pray.

Ah, God who lovest Thy creatures, sinful and poor
    and weak,
Hear'st prayer in the tired hearts throbbing, though
    the lips are too tired to speak?

Is this Thy answer? Is this the herald of Thy
    peace?
For the Lotus withers before him, the songs of the
    syrens cease.

And the palm trees and the grottoes, fountains and
    streamlets bright,
Waver and change as he cometh, then fade from our
    weary sight.

He is worn with care and labour; he is garbed in
    lowliest guise,
But we know the firm, sweet mouth, and the brave,
    brave patient eyes.

And we know the shining lilies — no blooms of
    mortal birth—
And we know thee, blessèd Joseph, in the guise that
    was thine on earth.

Thy hands are hardened with toil, but they have
    toiled for Him
Upon whose bidding waited legions of Seraphim.

Thy hands have trained to labour the hands of Him
    who made thee,
Whose strength upbore thy weakness when thy awful
    trust dismayed thee.

Oh, lift thy hands in appealing for us who, unwilling,
　　bear
The burden of God's belovèd, lowly labour and care.
Oh, pity our fruitless tears, to-night, and our hearts
　　too tired for prayer !

KATHERINE E. CONWAY.

SAINT JOSEPH'S DOUBT [1]

HOLY was good St. Joseph
　　When marrying Mary Mother ;
Surely his lot was happy,
　　Happy beyond all other.

Refusing red gold laid down,
　　And the crown by David worn,
With Mary to be abiding
　　And guiding her steps forlorn.

One day that the twain were talking,
　　And walking through gardens early,
Where cherries were redly growing,
　　And blossoms were blowing rarely,

[1] This is the Irish form of a legend which runs through the popular literature of nearly all countries. It is thus versified very literally from the Irish original by Dr. Douglas Hyde in his *Religious Songs of Connaught*. St. Joseph's perplexity regarded rather his own unworthiness to remain so close to One in whom some high supernatural mystery had been wrought : but we could not expect the subject to be treated in rustic ballads with the delicate accuracy of Father Januarius Bucceroni, S.J., in his chapter *De Solicitâ S. Josephi Cogitatione*.

Mary the fruit desired,
    For faint and tired she panted,
At the scent on the breeze's wing,
    Of the fruit that the King had planted.

Then spake to Joseph the Virgin,
    All weary and faint and low,
" Oh, pull me yon smiling cherries
    That fair on the tree do grow.

" For feeble I am, and weary,
    And my steps are but faint and slow,
And the works of the King of the graces
    I feel within me grow."

Then out spake the good St. Joseph,
    And stoutly indeed spake he,
" I shall not pluck thee one cherry,
    Who art untrue to me.

" Let him come fetch you the cherries,
    Who is dearer than I to thee."
Then Jesus, hearing St. Joseph,
    Thus spake to the stately tree,

" Bend low in her gracious presence,
    Stoop down to her, O tree,
That My Mother herself may pluck thee,
    And take thy burden from thee."

Then the great tree lowered her branches
  At hearing the high command,
And she plucked the fruit that it offered,
  Herself with her gentle hand.

Loud shouted the good St. Joseph,
  He cast himself on the ground,
"Go home and forgive me, Mary,
  To Jerusalem I am bound ;
I must go to the holy city,
  And confess my sin profound."

Then out spake the gentle Mary,
  She spake with a gentle voice,
"I shall not go home, O Joseph,
  But I bid thee at heart rejoice,
For the King of Heaven shall pardon
  The sin that was not of choice."

.   .   .   .

Three months from that self-same morning,
  The Blessèd Child was born,
Three kings did journey to worship
  That Babe from the lands of the morn.

Three months from that very evening,
  He was born there in a manger,
With asses, and kine, and bullocks,
  In the strange, cold place of a stranger.

Dr. Douglas Hyde.

SAINT JOSEPH'S WORKSHOP

THIS is St. Joseph's workshop—old and quaint!
So we will enter for a little space,
And watch with loving eyes our favourite Saint,
As to and fro he moves about the place.
His placid brow no trace of care betrays,
A heavenly look of peace is resting there,
How calm his face—how self-controlled his ways!
His very attitude suggests a prayer.

See how unceasingly he plies his trade;
His heavy saw is heard from hour to hour.
St. Joseph's work went well because he prayed:
Here is a lesson—*Prayer gives work its power!*
Labour and prayer his twin companions are,
And they are comrades also to us given:
Will they not sanctify, and lift us far
Above the snares that line our path to Heaven?

Within this workshop Jesus deigns to learn
How plane and saw and hammer should be used.
Well may our glowing hearts within us burn
While lessons of obedience are infused.
He, the Creator, does His creature's will,
Raises a plank or rests it on the sod.
But look at Joseph—oh, more wondrous still,
The creature ventures to command his God!

Beloved Saint, we venerate thee more,
As thus we ponder on thy sanctity;
For we can realise as ne'er before
How powerful must thy intercession be.
Help us, dear Father, as we humbly bend
To ask thy blessing on our daily life;
Be ever near us, even to the end,
And in temptation—aid us in the strife.

Holding thy hand, more firmly shall we tread,
Never one cry for help didst thou disdain:
The Saint of Carmel, St. Teresa, said
That she had never asked thy aid in vain.
Thou art the patron of a holy death,
To thee our last dread passage we confide;
Protect us to our latest dying breath—
Ah, *then* indeed, dear Saint, be near our side!

Ave M. C.

SAINT JOSEPH

To sing the praise of Mary's Spouse
And of that Galilean house,
White-walled, vine-garlanded,
Angel-encompassèd,
Might well a seraph's powers employ;
But as the shepherd-boy

To ease his spirit plies an oaten reed,
While, moving slow, the cropping wethers feed,
So I, in rude untutored verse,
Saint Joseph's worth rehearse.

And first, the Saint's thrice-holy dread
The spotless Maid to wed.
She of our tainted race
The one sole Miracle of Grace,
Predestined for the Spirit's Bride,
He thought to put aside.
Not long
Did Heaven permit unconscious wrong.
'Twas in a dream an angel spake,

" Joseph, fear not to take
Mary,"
And at th' angelic word
The Saint's strong faith, as did the Prophet's gourd,
Sprang vigorous in the night;
But no fierce sun by day could smite
Its spreading canopy.

One glorious burst of song,
Prophetic, strong,
Then silence golden as the pause between
Celestial melodies from choirs unseen,
Such was Our Lady's legacy;
But he

With never a word
The deeper silence stirred,
Pleased to play subject to so sweet a Queen.

    Engulfed in the white splendour,
At once so strong and tender,
Of his moon-sandalled Mate,[1]
What wonder that his high estate
Was dimly seen by mortal eyes!
For God is swift to teach, but man is slow to learn,
And the great truths we recognise
It took the race long centuries to discern.

    Dear Foster-Saint!
Thy earthly home knew little of earth's taint.
Though poor, it held earth's choicest treasures—
None other
Than sinless Babe and sinless Mother.
Patron of home and all its chastened pleasures!
Head of the family!
The favour that was thine
Win for us of thy boundless charity—
To breathe our souls out in the Arms Divine,
With Mary's prayerful eyes
Bent on us, shedding balm of Paradise.

                    T. H. WRIGHT.

[1] Apocalypse, xii. 1.

A FRIEND IN NEED

ACROSS a lonely country
  A weary woman speeds;
Her face is drawn in anguish,
  Her heart within her bleeds.

Behind her, on his pallet,
  So strangely still and wan,
Her little Joseph lieth,
  Her only darling son.

The light of life is fading
  Within his eyes so blue;
Upon his baby features
  The deathly ashen hue.

Why speeds the wretched mother
  Thus from her dying child,
Far through the deepening darkness,
  And tempest tossing wild?

On, on, through soaking pastures,
  On, up the mountain side,
With eyes so wildly straining,
  Her stumbling steps to guide.

"'Tis here, at last!" she murmurs,
  And how those poor eyes shine,
As on her knees she sinks, at
  A rude St. Joseph's shrine.

"O dear and kind St. Joseph!
    Thou Spouse of Mary mild;
Thou guide of little Jesus,
    Plead for my darling child.

"Pray thou the Lord of Glory—
    Since long ago thy Son,
Pray Him in love and pity
    To spare my little one."

Thus prays the trusting mother
    To that most holy Saint,
Who ever hears in pity
    A suffering parent's plaint.

Back through the night and tempest,
    With struggling, sobbing breath,
Her humble home she reaches:
    Is it the home of death?

With tortured, trembling fingers,
    She fumbles at the door;
Her heart beats nigh to bursting,
    Her pain is passing sore.

Before her, on his pallet,
    Her little Joseph lies;
But oh! dear heart! he knows her,
    A smile is in his eyes.

She sees the life-light shining,
   Those blue orbs free from pain,
And knows, in awe and wonder,
   Her boy is hers again.

Low on her knees, adoring,
   She sinks beside him there,
And thanks the Lord of Glory
   Who heard St. Joseph's prayer.

EMILY CHRISTIAN.

REVELATION IN DREAMS

THERE are who in the night lie down to slumber,
   And, waking, joy to know their grief a dream ;
   There are who wake and work beneath the gleam,
Yet, sleep—such fantasies their noonday cumber :
There is who, coming in the midnight sombre,
   Tells men of heaven beneath the clouds begun,
And bids them sorrows with their dreams to number,
   Which fade, and fading, bring to them the sun.
Sleep, sleep, O Joseph ; thou didst dream while
    waking,
   Thou in thy slumber things of day shalt hear ;

The star of morning says the day is breaking,
  The angel speaks the King of angels near.
O Foster-father, guard Thy household well—
The Ever-maiden, the Emmanuel.

ARTHUR M. MORGAN.

"FLY INTO EGYPT!"

To Egypt fly! Proud Herod's minions press.
  They seek the life of Him who came with cheer
  For sadden'd man, to light the darkness drear—
A Saviour born to ransom and to bless.
The faithful Joseph heard—with eagerness
  He fled with Maid and Child through lonely night,
  'Mid desert wastes—soul strengthen'd in the might
Of God's behest, and Child-God's sweet caress.
Through sunless tracts of toilsome, weary days,
  Life's duty leads us oft.   Where then the hope,
To steel our nerve or drooping courage raise,
  As through the tangled, darkling maze we grope?
Strong-rooted hope and fadeless joy are thine,
Companion of the Maid and Child Divine!

P. J. M'CURTIN, S.J.

MARY AND JOSEPH IN EGYPT

WHILST Joseph leads the patient beast and slow
   That bears the weight of Mary and her Son,
O'er rugged steeps, o'er barren plains they go,
   Through wildernesses till the day is done,
   Till 'neath the western wave hath set the sun.
Then, rest—till morning her bright face doth show ;
   Then, on again—their weary race is run.
They pass where stand in pride the idols : lo,
   A crash is heard.   In sudden ruin all
   Before the Sacred Infant headlong fall.
   Dog-faced Anubis, Isis too, the call,
The silent call obey, that given is now
By the Child-Saviour's mighty presence.   How
Doth joy celestial sit on Joseph's brow,
   While the meek Mother clasps her precious One !

ELLEN O'CONNELL FITZSIMON.

TO SAINT JOSEPH

BY Juda's olive-crowned and royal hills,
Of old there dwelt a man of kingly race,
Descendant of that line which ruled the land,
As by Judean streams years grew apace.

10

And he the guardian of a royal Maid
Was named by Heaven's Divine, all-wise command ;
O'er her, the flower of Israel's race, he watched
As seasons sped in Juda's smiling land.

Th' appointed time so long foretold is come :
Jehovah's chosen race with rapture thrills ;
The Christ of God, of Israel's God, is born,
The sun has risen o'er Judea's hills !

The old and simple tale we know full well,
The home at Nazareth, where, in times of yore,
The Holy Three in peace and love abode,
While summers waned and died on Juda's shore.

Far brighter than the day where no light falls,
There is a city of eternal rest,
Where Joseph pleads the cause of hearts sore tried,
Pleads from his throne amid the just made blest.

In Joseph all o'er-burdened souls find help,
To them his eyes with tender yearning turn ;
He hears their sighs, he listeth still their plaint,
While morn's glow pales, or night's star-fires do burn.

Great Pius lent this pillar to the Church—
" To Joseph go," as spake the king of yore ;
The people nearer still to Joseph draw,
Through coming ages shall, for evermore.

O Joseph! on this day, thy chosen one,
Though storms may rise and howling tempests rave,
Do thou look down upon our pilgrim souls,
And by thy power with Christ, in peril save.

Pray for the world, and for our Mother Church;
Pray for our lives, and all that they may hold;
Pray that our course may tend, by thorns or flowers,
Unto the jasper walls and streets of gold.

ANNA T. SADLIER.

A PICTURE OF SAINT JOSEPH

ROUND thy transparent forehead, gentle Saint,
No golden nimbus wreaths its mystic light,
And yet a radiance deeply, strangely bright
Is all about thee.   When did artist paint
Aught more ethereal than the lily skin,
Pure, fine and spotless as the soul within?
The wondrous texture of the soft white hair
Crowning a brow like marble clear and fair.

And as I gaze upon that noble face,
Time vanishes; again in Nazareth town
Those gentle, peaceful eyes are looking down,
Smiling at Jesus, in the little place

Ye both called home—your glimpse of heaven on
    earth;
For close beside she sits who gave Him birth,
Upon her lap some dainty work half done:
A lovely trio—happy three in one.

ANON.

THE RIVAL OF JOSEPH THE JUST

I HAVE not wearied you till now
    With prayers or praises, St. Matthias!
Nay, to my shame I must avow
    A lurking jealousy and bias.
For, though not yours the name whereby
    I'm known along life's dusty path, you
Have seemed unwittingly to vie
    With my true namesake, great St. Matthew.

Thus friends will wish me "happy feast"
    Your twenty-fourth of February,
Ere yet the frost and snow hath ceased,
    While sunbeams of their warmth are chary:
Whereas *my* patron's feast occurs
    The twenty-first of mild September,
Before the wintry tempest stirs,
    While fields the summer's heat remember.

Another prejudice I knew
   In childhood (pardon its survival!)—
Joseph the Just appeared for you
   A more than formidable rival.
Forgive me, humble Saint, if still
   The claims of Barsabas seem greater ;
But you, not he, were raised to fill
   The post left vacant by the Traitor.

I love him for his very name :
   Though name and nature often vary,
More than the name could Joseph claim
   Of likeness to the Spouse of Mary.
God's Word confirms the people's word
   When (like his namesake) "*just*" they called him ;[1]
Yet you before him were preferred,
   And in Apostle's place forestalled him.

Great, then, your virtues must have been,
   And great must be your heavenly glory,
Matthias, though so dense a screen
   Hides almost all your earthly story.
Nothing is known save this alone—
   God joined you to the great Eleven
On earth, and an Apostle's throne
   Is yours for ever now in heaven.

                    MATTHEW RUSSELL, S.J.

[1] Matt. i. 19 ; Acts i. 23.

A PRAYER TO SAINT JOSEPH

I'VE a favour, dear St. Joseph,
  That I long to ask of thee,
And 'twill make me good and happy
  If thou'lt grant it unto me.

Help me ever to remember
  That God sees me all the time—
From the first faint dawn of morning
  Till the evening *Aves* chime ;

And that even in the darkness
  Does the eye of God behold
All the thoughts and all the actions
  Of each lamb of His great fold.

Thus I'm certain, dear St. Joseph,
  I shall ever careful be
Not to have a thing about me
  That Our Lord would grieve to see.

ANON.

SAINT JOSEPH AND THE PRESENCE LIGHT

THERE is a brightness lovelier than the day,
  A lamp whose shining is as mystic wine,
Melting all sadness from the heart away,
  And wakening thought and hope of joys divine.

For where it ever burneth 'tis the sign
Of presence true of Him who loves to dwell
    Amongst the sons of men ; nor palace fine
Nor royal state demands, but one small cell
Where they may find Him and adore, who love
        Him well.

Like to this lamp, the memory is of him
    By wondrous favour set to ward and tend
God's living ark, more pure than Seraphim,
    And God Himself incarnate ; thus to spend
    His humble life obscure ; to shape and mend
And build, and wearily at eve sit down,
    With Christ and Mary, father, husband, friend,
While each would kiss his face sunburnt and brown,
And smooth his stiffened hands, and care in full bliss
        drown.

So Joseph's name brings up sweet thoughts afresh
    Of earth's most blissful days, when seen and felt
Our Life Divine did human life refresh
    At Mary's virgin breasts, or kingly dealt
    Largess of rapture to the few who knelt
In faith adoring ; till our hearts, still clinging
    To human love, in love Divine do melt,
And hasten we to where, warm radiance flinging,
The Bridegroom's lamp says : " Hither come, your
        best love bringing."

ANON.

THE SUFFRAGES OF SAINT JOSEPH

(FROM THE ROMAN BREVIARY)

At Vespers.

Lo, the faithful, prudent servant
    O'er God's household who presides ;
In his home are glory, riches,
    And his justice aye abides.

At Lauds.

THIRTY years was Christ reputed
    Son of Joseph pure and meek.
Wisdom shall the just one ponder,
    And his tongue shall judgment speak.

Let us pray.

O GOD, who through Thy providence serene
    Hast deigned to choose St. Joseph as the Spouse
Of Thy most Holy Mother, and our Queen,
    Hear, we implore Thee, hear our prayers and vows !
Grant, we beseech Thee, gracious Lord ! that he
    Whom here on earth we venerate and love
As our protector, may for ever be
    Our intercessor near Thy throne above.

                         M. R.

SAINT JOSEPH

ST. JOSEPH, lineal son of kings,
Thy hands are set to lowly things;
But oh, thy spirit upward wings
  To David's kingdom true.
Oh, get us grace to labour here
With hearts above this earthly sphere,
Fixed in that home we're drawing near
  By evil days and few.

St. Joseph, rising in the night,
And o'er the desert taking flight,
To save from cruel Herod's might
  The Mother and her Son.
Oh, may we promptly night and day
God's angel messengers obey,
And cheerfully without delay
  To do His bidding run.

Oh, great St. Joseph, humble, mild,
Spouse of the Virgin undefiled,
Dear Foster-father of her Child,
  How high a lot was thine!
And yet how humble was thy heart!
Oh, teach us all the holy art
To act with fervent zeal our part,
  Then trust in power Divine.

St. Joseph, by thy passage blest
From labour to eternal rest,
Thy agèd head on Jesus' breast,
    And Mary's hands in thine.
Oh, come and help us all to die,
With Mary and her Son be nigh,
And bid Hell's darksome shadows fly,
    And Heaven's calm light outshine!

SISTER MARY STANISLAUS MacCARTHY, O.S.D.

SAINT JOSEPH

WHEN the people of Egypt of food stood in need,
They went to King Pharaoh, their sovereign, to plead,
To ask him for bread, lest their children should
    die:
"Go to Joseph for succour," was Pharaoh's reply.

King Pharaoh, of Egypt the ruler and king,
Raised up the wise Joseph and gave him his ring,
And a robe and a chain with his own royal hand,
And made him a ruler all over the land.

And Joseph stored up an abundance of bread,
With which during famine the people were fed,
And by this was prefigured that Bread from on high
Which is broken to us every day lest we die.

The true Bread of Life which my loving Lord gave,
The night ere He died and was laid in the grave,
Was preserved by St. Joseph, whom holy we name,
And whom as their patron all Catholics claim.

The High King of heaven made him ruler on earth,
To guard Heaven's Queen and to tend from His birth
Our Saviour, our King, our great High Priest and
    Head,
Who indeed of our souls is the Life-giving Bread.

That Bread ever holy, soul-saving, and sweet,
He gave His disciples, saying, " Take ye and eat,
For this is My body "—and so *we* believe
Who His Body and Blood at the altar receive.

O holy St. Joseph, to whom it was given
To have in thy charge all the riches of Heaven,
Obtain I may worthily eat of that Bread
To preserve which, with Mary, to Egypt you fled.

Chaste Spouse of the Virgin, St. Joseph the just,
Great on earth were thy virtues, and great was thy
    trust ;
And great is thy glory, thy well-earnèd meed,
And great is thy power to help us in need.

Thy virtues were crowned with the happiest death,
When Jesus was near thee to catch thy last breath,

And Mary, His Mother, had knelt by thy side,
How happy and holy, dear Patron, you died!

Ah, dear holy Patron, your client defend,
When he, a poor sinner, approaches his end ;
Drive away all the demons surrounding his bed,
And strengthen his soul with the Life-giving Bread.

Obtain that a priest may be found by his side
To give him his Lord as his sins are untied,
And His image, the crucifix, press to his lips
Ere his reason shall suffer a lasting eclipse.

Obtain that the angels may come to his aid
To guard him when most of dread judgment afraid,
That he may as a fervent poor penitent die,
And go after death to the mansions on high.

REV. JAMES CASEY

THE DEATH OF SAINT JOSEPH.

A SIMPLE print, from hand of high renown,
Upon my low bed's head looks kindly down ;
—The Patriarch Joseph, Foster-father mild
Of Nazareth's Virgin Mother's heavenly Child ;

His dying head pressed close against the knee
Of the Incarnate Son and Deity ;—
The Virgin Mother kneeling gently near,
Dissolved in prayer, on that mild cheek a tear ;—
Thus has the Christian Master's pious mind,
Great Overbeck, the " just man's " death designed.
The picture, breathing all the holy peace
Of souls which find in death, from death, release,
Thus placed, a wish long cherished found expression—
When I shall come to my death-bed confession ;
When faithful priest shall that last unction give
Which bids these lapsing, dying senses live
On God's own day of happy resurrection,
As long-tried vessels of most sweet election ;
When on my parched, enfeebled tongue shall lie
Jesus Himself, in loving mystery ;
Then may three friends, in fair, celestial state,
Unseen, around my bed benignly wait ;
Thus shall I win, while yielding up my breath,
Life's last and crowning grace, a happy death.

O Jesus, Mary, Joseph ! thus I sigh
Each night as 'neath that picture's wing I lie ;
O Jesus, Mary, Joseph ! me befriend
When this so troubled life begins to end ;
O Jesus, Mary, Joseph ! with you near,
Death's dreaded spectres all will disappear ;

And though no friend may come with pious care
To wipe the death-sweat, lift the last sweet prayer,
Contentedly, serenely, I can die
In your most dear and holy company.

ELIZA ALLEN STARR.

———

SAINT JOSEPH'S CROWN

THE princes of this earth!   If princely power
   Be measured by the wealth and might of them
   Who own a monarch's sway, thy diadem
Is worth a thousand crowns ; the lordliest tower,
To thy poor cot, scarce proof against a shower,
   Were as a pebble to some priceless gem ;
   For there from Jesse's root the lily stem
Blossomed unseen and bore the promised flower.
There didst thou guard the mother and her boy,
   The Virgin Mother and her Babe Divine,
Sharing each solemn grief, each sacred joy,
   Ruling the little house, for at a sign
Jesus obeyed.   Ah, there is no alloy
   In such a crown, and, Joseph, it is thine !

C. W. BARRAUD, S.J

———

A NOVEL PLEA

When Joseph's Foster-Son my judge shall be,
   I'll urge a claim unknown in eschatology—
O dear St. Joseph, won't you plead for me,
   The first compiler of your own Anthology?[1]

[1] There are many books of verse in French and in Italian, and perhaps in other languages, devoted exclusively to the praise of St. Joseph, such as the *Canzoniere di San Giuseppe* of Father Jerome Raffo, S.J.; but *Saint Joseph's Anthology*, to which these last pages are an appendix, seems to be the first and only book which gathers into one all the tributes paid to the holy Patriarch by an entire literature. The preceding twenty-four poems, added to those contained in the *Anthology*, brings the total number up to one hundred and forty-two.

M. H. GILL AND SON, DUBLIN.

COMPILED BY THE AUTHOR OF THIS VOLUME,

Price Three Shillings,

Saint Joseph's Anthology:

Poems in praise of the Foster-Father, gathered from Various Sources.

Besides appreciative reviews in the Catholic journals on both sides of the Atlantic (*Tablet, Boston Pilot, Weekly Register, New Ireland Review, Ave Maria, Freeman's Journal, Irish Rosary, Irish Catholic,* and even the more worldly *Irish Figaro*), favourable notices appeared in *The Athenæum, The Illustrated London News, The Speaker,* etc. The last-named of these gave the following criticism :—

"'Saint Joseph's Anthology' is, as its name implies, a gathering together of poems in honour of the Foster-father of Jesus. The Editor has done his work devoutly and with diligence. From Father Southwell to Keble, from St. Alphonsus Liguori to Newman, is a wide field, but it has been carefully picked. Aubrey de Vere contributes a notably exquisite slice of a book which is rightly simple in much of its contents. Contributors are far from being limited to the Church which makes a special cult of St. Joseph : the humblest and most hidden of all Saints would seem to have a larger Protestant *clientèle* than one suspected. As mere poets, Father Russell's contributors who rank highest are, besides the illustrious names quoted above, Rosa Mulholland, John Boyle O'Reilly, Rose Kavanagh, Rev. Clarence Walworth, Rev. John Fitzpatrick, the Editor, and of course Father Faber. But it is hardly a book to be judged from a merely literary standpoint. Unction, grace, unworldliness, and fervour contribute to much excellent hymn-writing, and a book not one item of which is wholly unworthy."

www.ingramcontent.com/pod-product-compliance
Lightning Source LLC
Chambersburg PA
CBHW021117020726
47500CB00003B/800